T0254224

Practical Linux Topics

Chris Binnie

Apress®

Practical Linux Topics

Copyright © 2016 by Chris Binnie

This work is subject to copyright. All rights are reserved by the Publisher, whether the whole or part of the material is concerned, specifically the rights of translation, reprinting, reuse of illustrations, recitation, broadcasting, reproduction on microfilms or in any other physical way, and transmission or information storage and retrieval, electronic adaptation, computer software, or by similar or dissimilar methodology now known or hereafter developed. Exempted from this legal reservation are brief excerpts in connection with reviews or scholarly analysis or material supplied specifically for the purpose of being entered and executed on a computer system, for exclusive use by the purchaser of the work. Duplication of this publication or parts thereof is permitted only under the provisions of the Copyright Law of the Publisher's location, in its current version, and permission for use must always be obtained from Springer. Permissions for use may be obtained through RightsLink at the Copyright Clearance Center. Violations are liable to prosecution under the respective Copyright Law.

ISBN-13 (pbk): 978-1-4842-1771-9

IISBN-13 (electronic): 978-1-4842-1772-6

Trademarked names, logos, and images may appear in this book. Rather than use a trademark symbol with every occurrence of a trademarked name, logo, or image we use the names, logos, and images only in an editorial fashion and to the benefit of the trademark owner, with no intention of infringement of the trademark.

The use in this publication of trade names, trademarks, service marks, and similar terms, even if they are not identified as such, is not to be taken as an expression of opinion as to whether or not they are subject to proprietary rights.

While the advice and information in this book are believed to be true and accurate at the date of publication, neither the authors nor the editors nor the publisher can accept any legal responsibility for any errors or omissions that may be made. The publisher makes no warranty, express or implied, with respect to the material contained herein.

Managing Director: Welmoed Spahr
Lead Editor: Louise Corrigan
Development Editor: James Markham
Technical Reviewer: Sander van Vugt
Editorial Board: Steve Anglin, Pramila Balen, Louise Corrigan, Jim DeWolf, Jonathan Gennick, Robert Hutchinson, Celestin Suresh John, Michelle Lowman, James Markham, Susan McDermott, Matthew Moodie, Jeffrey Pepper, Douglas Pundick, Ben Renow-Clarke, Gwenan Spearing
Coordinating Editor: Jill Balzano
Copy Editor: Kezia Endsley
Compositor: SPi Global
Indexer: SPi Global
Artist: SPi Global

Distributed to the book trade worldwide by Springer Science+Business Media New York, 233 Spring Street, 6th Floor, New York, NY 10013. Phone 1-800-SPRINGER, fax (201) 348-4505, e-mail orders-ny@springer-sbm.com, or visit www.springeronline.com. Apress Media, LLC is a California LLC and the sole member (owner) is Springer Science + Business Media Finance Inc (SSBM Finance Inc). SSBM Finance Inc is a Delaware corporation.

For information on translations, please e-mail rights@apress.com, or visit www.apress.com.

Apress and friends of ED books may be purchased in bulk for academic, corporate, or promotional use. eBook versions and licenses are also available for most titles. For more information, reference our Special Bulk Sales–eBook Licensing web page at www.apress.com/bulk-sales.

Any source code or other supplementary material referenced by the author in this text is available to readers at www.apress.com/. For detailed information about how to locate your book's source code, go to www.apress.com/source-code/.

*Dedicated to systems that say, without providing any other details,
"There has been an error", my long-suffering better half, and my two beautiful children,
without whom this book would have been finished earlier.*

Contents at a Glance

Contents

About the Author

Chris Binnie is a technical consultant who has worked online with Linux systems for almost two decades. During his travels he has deployed many servers in the Cloud and on banking and government server estates. As well as building an Autonomous System Network in 2005 and serving HD video to 77 countries via a media streaming platform, which he architected and built, he has written for *Linux Magazine* and *Admin Magazine* for a number of years. Outside of work, Chris enjoys the outdoors, watching Liverpool FC, and extolling the virtues of the ever-flawless Ockham's Razor.

About the Technical Reviewer

Sander van Vugt is a Linux expert working from the Netherlands as an author, technical trainer, and consultant for clients around the world. Sander has published several books about different Linux distributions and is a regular contributor to major international Linux-related web sites. As a consultant, he specializes in Linux high availability and performance optimization. As a technical trainer, Sander is an authorized trainer for SUSE Linux Enterprise Server and Red Hat Enterprise Linux. More information about him can be found on his web site at `www.sandervanvugt.com`.

Introduction

Almost all of the world's supercomputers and even the International Space Station use a powerful, efficient operating system called Linux. In addition, the vast majority of smart phones and embedded devices on the planet, such as broadband routers and boxes connected to televisions, use Linux. This book examines a number of diverse, server-related subjects that you can learn and then reference again later.

A common misconception is that specializing in a single systems area is sufficient, but in my experience every technical role demands a different set of skills because each organization uses a unique combination of software. The aim of this book is to explore many different subjects and present them in such a way that technical people from all walks of life, whether they be sysadmins, developers, or devops engineers, will benefit.

Ultimately, however, this book is a celebration of the combined efforts of the community-spirited people who give us Linux which, whether we realize it or not, almost all of us use in one way or another on a daily basis.

■ ■ ■

## CHAPTER 1

Real-Time Network Statistics with Iftop

Monitoring network connections certainly can be frustrating, mainly because they can be established and then disappear within a matter of seconds. In this chapter, I show you how to achieve a Zen-like approach to monitoring network connections on your servers using a command line–based tool called iftop. I then finish by walking through the creation of a configuration file that you can use again on different servers once you have your monitoring set up as you prefer.

Monitoring Network Connections with netstat

The netstat command-line tool has been a staple among system admins. Although rich in features, including an auto-refresh parameter (continuous mode), netstat is certainly not designed to do much more than output raw numbers and names (from hosts and ports). To run netstat in continuous mode, for example, you can use:

```
# netstat -c
```

I usually end up running it alongside watch to give me the kind of clean screen refreshes I need for different scenarios; for example:

```
# watch -n2 "netstat -tu"
```

In this example, watch lets me configure a two-second gap prior to running the command again and updating its output (see Figure 1-1).

```
Active Internet connections (w/o servers)
Proto Recv-Q Send-Q Local Address              Foreign Address        State
tcp        0      0 Mia:35147                  host162-rangeA-go:https ESTABLISHED
tcp        0      0 Mia:58928                  host227-rangeB-go:https ESTABLISHED
tcp        0      0 Mia:53135                  cb-in-f120.1e100.:https ESTABLISHED
tcp        0      0 Mia:39854                  lhr08s05-in-f234.:https TIME_WAIT
tcp        0      0 Mia:51598                  host226-rangeB-go:https TIME_WAIT
tcp        0      0 Mia:33247                  wm-in-f188.1e100.n:5228 ESTABLISHED
tcp        0      0 Mia:49143                  host232-rangeB-go:https ESTABLISHED
tcp        0      0 Mia:48546                  host183-rangeA-go:https ESTABLISHED
tcp        0      0 Mia:60490                  lhr08s06-in-f5.1e:https ESTABLISHED
tcp        0      0 Mia:54672                  host242-rangeB-go:https ESTABLISHED
udp        0      0 Mia:57764                  lax17s04-in-f3.1e:https ESTABLISHED
udp        0      0 Mia:34254                  wa-in-f189.1e100.:https ESTABLISHED
udp        0      0 Mia:36933                  wl-in-f189.1e100.:https ESTABLISHED
```

Figure 1-1. *The "watch" command executing "netstat -tu" every two seconds*

In this scenario, the -tu switch tells netstat to output both TCP and UDP statistics. Using the watch option is far slicker than the continuous -c parameter, because it adds information to the foot of the last output, although the output is still a little messy and difficult to follow. Incidentally, the following netstat command is the one I use the most:

```
# netstat -tulpnc
```

In Figure 1-2, I ask netstat to show all local listening ports and then the processes that they belong to. However, lsof -i, a command concerned with listing open files, is probably more effective.

```
Active Internet connections (w/o servers)
Proto Recv-Q Send-Q Local Address          Foreign Address       State
tcp       0      0 Mia:53135               cb-in-f120.1e100.:https ESTABLISHED
tcp       0      0 Mia:43711               lhr08s07-in-f33.1:https ESTABLISHED
tcp       0      0 Mia:33247               wm-in-f188.1e100.n:5228 ESTABLISHED
tcp       0      0 Mia:49143               host232-rangeB-go:https ESTABLISHED
tcp       0      0 Mia:48546               host183-rangeA-go:https ESTABLISHED
tcp       0      0 Mia:41018               lhr14s27-in-f1.1e:https ESTABLISHED
tcp       0      0 Mia:60490               lhr08s06-in-f5.1e:https ESTABLISHED
tcp       0      0 Mia:54672               host242-rangeB-go:https ESTABLISHED
udp       0      0 Mia:36933               wl-in-f189.1e100.:https ESTABLISHED
udp       0      0 Mia:54593               lk-in-f94.1e100.n:https ESTABLISHED
Active Internet connections (w/o servers)
Proto Recv-Q Send-Q Local Address          Foreign Address       State
tcp       0      0 Mia:53135               cb-in-f120.1e100.:https ESTABLISHED
tcp       0      0 Mia:43711               lhr08s07-in-f33.1:https ESTABLISHED
tcp       0      0 Mia:33247               wm-in-f188.1e100.n:5228 ESTABLISHED
tcp       0      0 Mia:49143               host232-rangeB-go:https ESTABLISHED
tcp       0      0 Mia:48546               host183-rangeA-go:https ESTABLISHED
tcp       0      0 Mia:41018               lhr14s27-in-f1.1e:https ESTABLISHED
tcp       0      0 Mia:60490               lhr08s06-in-f5.1e:https ESTABLISHED
tcp       0      0 Mia:54672               host242-rangeB-go:https ESTABLISHED
udp       0      0 Mia:36933               wl-in-f189.1e100.:https ESTABLISHED
udp       0      0 Mia:54593               lk-in-f94.1e100.n:https ESTABLISHED
Active Internet connections (w/o servers)
Proto Recv-Q Send-Q Local Address          Foreign Address       State
tcp       0      0 Mia:53135               cb-in-f120.1e100.:https ESTABLISHED
tcp       0      0 Mia:43711               lhr08s07-in-f33.1:https ESTABLISHED
tcp       0      0 Mia:33247               wm-in-f188.1e100.n:5228 ESTABLISHED
tcp       0      0 Mia:49143               host232-rangeB-go:https ESTABLISHED
tcp       0      0 Mia:48546               host183-rangeA-go:https ESTABLISHED
tcp       0      0 Mia:41018               lhr14s27-in-f1.1e:https ESTABLISHED
tcp       0      0 Mia:60490               lhr08s06-in-f5.1e:https ESTABLISHED
tcp       0      0 Mia:54672               host242-rangeB-go:https ESTABLISHED
udp       0      0 Mia:36933               wl-in-f189.1e100.:https ESTABLISHED
udp       0      0 Mia:54593               lk-in-f94.1e100.n:https ESTABLISHED
```

Figure 1-2. "netstat" output displays changing information by repeating the output at the foot of the screen upon refresh

Introducing iftop

Thankfully, there's a utility that takes away painful eyestrain: iftop (http://www.ex-parrot.com/pdw/iftop/). iftop is to networks what top is to CPUs. And, in the same way ifconfig refers to configuring an interface, the friendly iftop stands for "interface top".

The main difference between iftop and other command line–based tools is that iftop instantly draws highly useful bar graphs (among other graphical options) and I can't emphasize enough how many times it has saved the day when diagnosing an urgent server or network issue.

The fact that there's no pained preamble with device drivers or libraries—iftop "just works"—makes all the difference when you're in a hurry. Its small footprint might also be helpful in diagnosing a customer server that doesn't have iftop installed: the tiny package can be easily dropped on a memory stick when the networking is broken on the problematic server.

Installing iftop

On Debian-based systems, you can install iftop with the following command:

```
# apt-get install iftop
```

On Red Hat derivatives, you can install the EPEL (Extra Packages for Enterprise Linux) RPM, using for example:

```
# rpm -ivh http://download.fedoraproject.org/pub/epel/6/i386/epel-release-6-8.noarch.rpm
```

For older versions of the Red Hat family, you can follow the instructions at http://www.cyberciti.biz/faq/fedora-sl-centos-redhat6-enable-epel-repo/.
You should then be able to install iftop as usual:

```
# yum install iftop
```

If you execute iftop with just an interface to examine, you can spawn it using the following command:

```
# iftop -i eth0
```

Figure 1-3 shows a sample output of this command. The output shows a number of remote hosts (including nicknames added to the file /etc/hosts, as well as fully qualified domain names, which are really just normal hostnames that I've abbreviated) in the middle column and the local machine named Sula in the left column.

```
                  19.1Mb            38.1Mb           57.2Mb           76.3Mb            95.4Mb
    |               |                 |                |                |                 |
Mia                            => caesar.acc.umu.se               190Kb    203Kb    193Kb
███████████                    <=                               10.7Mb   10.6Mb   10.3Mb
Mia                            => nrt13s18-in-f31.1e100.net          0b    3.35Kb    868b
                               <=                                    0b    3.57Kb    925b
Mia                            => host183-rangeA-google-ggc.cdn.thlon.isp.s  0b 1.74Kb 1.19Kb
                               <=                                    0b    0.99Kb    434b
Mia                            => wl-in-f189.1e100.net            2.00Kb    410b     205b
                               <=                                 1.29Kb    265b     253b
Mia                            => host237-rangeB-google-ggc.cdn.thlon.isp.s 208b  42b   21b
                               <=                                  844b     169b     53b
Mia                            => wq-in-f189.1e100.net               0b      42b    113b
                               <=                                    0b      50b    138b
Mia                            => host162-rangeA-google-ggc.cdn.thlon.isp.s 208b  42b  10b
                               <=                                  208b      42b     10b
Mia                            => host242-rangeB-google-ggc.cdn.thlon.isp.s   0b  42b  10b
                               <=                                    0b      42b     10b
Mia                            => wm-in-f188.1e100.net               0b      42b     10b
                               <=                                    0b      42b     10b
Mia                            => lhr14s24-in-f69.1e100.net          0b       0b     10b
                               <=                                    0b       0b     10b
Mia                            => host232-rangeB-google-ggc.cdn.thlon.isp.s  0b   0b   10b
                               <=                                    0b       0b     10b

TX:           cum:   1.19MB   peak:   232Kb                rates:    192Kb    209Kb    195Kb
RX:                  62.3MB          10.7Mb                          10.7Mb   10.6Mb   10.3Mb
TOTAL:               63.4MB          10.9Mb                          10.9Mb   10.8Mb   10.4Mb
```

Figure 1-3. *The default "iftop -i eth0" output listening to an interface enabled*

On the right side, you can see three columns. The excellent iftop refers to this as its *display order* and the columns deal with different time-delay averages. By default, this appears (at least) to be two-second, ten-second, and forty-second averages. These values can be configured separately, so don't let that confuse you too much initially. In addition, it's easy to change the overall display using those columns by pressing the 1, 2, or 3 keys to respectively filter by the aforementioned 2s, 10s, or 40s averages.

As an aside, a two-second average is really short; I love it having come from a background filled with what felt like lengthy five-minute SNMP averages. I can see very quickly what's just changed on the network and although two seconds isn't real-time, it's very close to it and certainly has its place on today's busy Internet. I find that it's just long enough for you to be able to spot something without worrying about freezing the screen in case you missed it.

When you're running the default config without specifying any options, iftop outputs the busiest hosts in the last ten seconds (in other words, by using a ten-second average). It also groups hosts in pairs to choose the busiest *pair* of combined inbound and outbound traffic.

Finally, at the end of the output, you are presented with a number of totals. These include useful statistics, such as the amount of data transferred in megabytes (MB) as well as forty-second averages of traffic, usually in megabits (Mb), but also sometimes in *kb* for kilobytes.

Controlling iftop from the Keyboard

In addition to providing a slick graphical display, even through an SSH terminal, iftop lets you modify your configuration at the press of a key. For example, in the course of a sysadmin's work day, you could be checking all sorts of bad networking habits: from monitoring the misconfiguration of a network interface to mitigating a hideously hazardous ARP storm. With iftop, you can cycle through a number of options and confidently choose a config parameter to suit your current scenario instantly.

Here are some examples of how iftop can make your sysadmin life easier at the press of key:

- To change the source and destination displays, press the *s* key or the *d* key while iftop is running. This helps isolate who is sending what, especially if iftop is being run on a Linux router (which I'll touch in "Using iftop on Busy Routers" later in this chapter) and forwarding traffic.

- To quickly see which ports are in use, press the *p* key. You can also use the Shift+S and Shift+D keys to expose source and destination ports, respectively. Figure 1-4 demonstrates how friendly iftop is with its options and how it dutifully reports, in the top-left of the screen, the result of the keypress that it has just received.

- To cycle through several different displays (similar to horizontal bar graphs), press the *t* key.

```
 Port display SOURCE    195Kb          391Kb          586Kb          781Kb               977Kb
                         |              |              |              |                   |
Mia:56760                    => wk-in-f189.1e100.net:https                 0b      313b    214b
                             <=                                            0b      270b    175b
Mia:58604                    => lhr14s23-in-f14.1e100.net:https            0b       42b     10b
                             <=                                            0b       42b     10b
Mia:58608                    => lhr14s23-in-f14.1e100.net:https          208b       42b     10b
                             <=                                          208b       42b     10b
Mia:40704                    => dfw06s38-in-f24.1e100.net:https            0b        0b    419b
                             <=                                            0b        0b    338b
Mia:50806                    => wl-in-f188.1e100.net:https                 0b        0b     26b
                             <=                                            0b        0b     15b
Mia:34791                    => lhr14s23-in-f37.1e100.net:https            0b        0b     10b
                             <=                                            0b        0b     10b
Mia:50232                    => dfw06s38-in-f24.1e100.net:https            0b        0b     10b
                             <=                                            0b        0b     10b




TX:        cum:    658KB  peak:   8.19Kb              rates:    208b    396b    701b
RX:                1.71MB         6.60Kb                        208b    353b    570b
TOTAL:             2.35MB         14.8Kb                        416b    749b    1.24Kb
```

Figure 1-4. *This output shows all the ports that are visible and an option selection, top-left*

Earlier, in Figure 1-3, you saw the standard two-line display. Its purpose might not be entirely obvious however because there's little-to-no traffic moving between hosts (so the white bars, like a bar graph, aren't present), but you can see the => and <= symbols depicting the direction of the traffic.

Figure 1-5 shows a nice feature that is useful in some circumstances. The single line-per-host display (showing both <= and => directions on one line) means that it's easy to spot who is hogging your bandwidth. Figure 1-6 informs you who is moving the most outbound traffic with a single => directional pointer. These two options (the aggregation of inbound and outbound traffic onto one line and choosing a particular direction that you're interested in) are best suited for very busy networks.

```
                 12.5Kb            25.0Kb            37.5Kb            50.0Kb            62.5Kb
 L_____|_____|_____|_____|_____
 Mia:56760                  <=> wk-in-f189.1e100.net                              0b    110b    389b
 Mia:47853                  <=> wk-in-f93.1e100.net                             416b     83b     21b
 Mia:33865                  <=> lhr14s27-in-f14.1e100.net                       416b     83b     21b
 Mia:51414                  <=> wj-in-f94.1e100.net                               0b      0b  1.14Kb
 Mia:58098                  <=> lhr14s23-in-f37.1e100.net                         0b      0b  1.13Kb
 Mia:34798                  <=> lhr14s23-in-f37.1e100.net                         0b      0b    491b
 Mia:51307                  <=> lhr14s23-in-f46.1e100.net                         0b      0b    328b
 Mia:59528                  <=> fra07s28-in-f24.1e100.net                         0b      0b     86b
 Mia:50806                  <=> wl-in-f188.1e100.net                              0b      0b     41b
 Mia:58661                  <=> lhr14s23-in-f46.1e100.net                         0b      0b     21b
 Mia:34983                  <=> lhr14s23-in-f3.1e100.net                          0b      0b     21b



 _____
 TX:           cum:   145KB  peak:   16.6Kb                    rates:   416b    138b  2.13Kb
 RX:                 83.0KB          17.5Kb                             416b    138b  1.52Kb
 TOTAL:               228KB          32.1Kb                             832b    277b  3.65Kb
```

Figure 1-5. *Traffic is displayed with both hosts occupying one line*

```
                 12.5Kb            25.0Kb            37.5Kb            50.0Kb            62.5Kb
 L_____|_____|_____|_____|_____
 Mia:56760                  => wk-in-f189.1e100.net                               0b     55b     51b
 Mia:50806                  => wl-in-f188.1e100.net                               0b     42b     10b
 Mia:47616                  => lhr14s23-in-f46.1e100.net                          0b      0b  12.3Kb
 Mia:54599                  => fra07s63-in-f15.1e100.net                          0b      0b    832b
 Mia:48382                  => lhr14s23-in-f46.1e100.net                          0b      0b    578b
 Mia:58662                  => lhr14s23-in-f46.1e100.net                          0b      0b    395b
 Mia:42036                  => fra07s63-in-f15.1e100.net                          0b      0b    275b
 Mia:51851                  => routerlogin.net                                    0b      0b     15b
 Mia:18994                  => routerlogin.net                                    0b      0b     12b
 Mia:58661                  => lhr14s23-in-f46.1e100.net                          0b      0b     10b
 Mia:34983                  => lhr14s23-in-f3.1e100.net                           0b      0b     10b



 _____
 TX:           cum:   223KB  peak:    236Kb                    rates:     0b     97b  14.5Kb
 RX:                  104KB           39.4Kb                              0b     97b  3.49Kb
 TOTAL:               328KB            249Kb                              0b    194b  17.9Kb
```

Figure 1-6. *Here "iftop" shows "sent" traffic only. The next selectable option is "received" traffic only*

Adding Screen Filters

The purpose of the *screen filter* is to tidy up a screen that is far too busy to keep track of. Imagine, for example, that you check your network connections and suddenly spot a host that looks suspicious. In that case, quickly press *P* to pause (or freeze) the ever-changing display and then the *l* key, followed by the hostname, which you've just spotted to add a screen filter. That way, the trusty iftop only passes back the connection information for that host on its own for closer inspection.

Figure 1-7 shows iftop asking for the *screen filter* phrase or keyword to match, in the top left of the screen. If it's a tricky IP address or long hostname, then you should be able to cut and paste into that field.

```
Screen filter> routerlogin
Mia                         => lhr14s23-in-f14.1e100.net        0b    3.50Kb   2.92Kb
                            <=                                   0b    2.70Kb   2.25Kb
Mia                         => fra07s63-in-f15.1e100.net        0b    3.25Kb   2.70Kb
                            <=                                   0b    2.50Kb   2.08Kb
Mia                         => routerlogin.net                  0b     347b     289b
                            <=                                   0b     580b     483b
Mia                         => wk-in-f189.1e100.net             0b      97b      81b
                            <=                                   0b     104b      87b
Mia                         => wl-in-f188.1e100.net             0b      42b      35b
                            <=                                   0b      42b      35b
Mia                         => lhr14s23-in-f5.1e100.net         0b      42b      35b
                            <=                                   0b      42b      35b



TX:              cum:   9.08KB  peak:   18.8Kb            rates:    0b   7.26Kb   6.05Kb
RX:                     7.43KB          15.6Kb                      0b   5.95Kb   4.96Kb
TOTAL:                  16.5KB          34.4Kb                      0b   13.2Kb   11.0Kb
```

Figure 1-7. *Filter that screen output to make more sense of it with a "screen filter"*

One key difference between other filters and a screen filter is that the totals at the bottom of the screen are not affected by any screen-filtering functionality.

Using Regular Expressions

Iftop also supports regular expressions, otherwise known as regex, following the POSIX format. The man page offers an excellent filter, if not one that's slightly more complicated than others, to get you started with some of the ways that you can manipulate iftop:

```
not ether host ff:ff:ff:ff:ff:ff
```

This very useful filter ignores all broadcast packets. Such a filter, like all others incidentally, can equally be applied as a screen filter with the letter *l* or the letter *f* as a live filter change to the currently enabled net filter. Alternatively, you can add it on the command line at launch time as well as in the start-up configuration file (which I will look at further in a moment). By removing broadcast traffic, you are effectively sorting the wheat from the chaff so that you can focus on the connections on your server directly and not the normally non-trivial amount of network noise filling your screen up with connections.

iftop also accepts regular expressions in the same way that ngrep or tcpdump do; for example:

```
port smtp and host mail.chrisbinnie.tld
```

If I wanted to monitor traffic to my mail server but avoid all SMTP traffic (which uses TCP port 25), I could use the and and not operators like this:

```
host mail.chrisbinnie.tld and not port 25
```

■ **Note**   As you're probably aware, Linux will look up the file /etc/services to match port numbers against service names. If you don't know which port number a service uses, you can query that file to find out.

As mentioned, these filters can be run in a variety of ways, including from the command line as follows at execution time, saving you typing time with the following syntax:

```
# iftop -f "host mail.chrisbinnie.tld and not port smtp"
```

This startup configuration simply checks for all traffic (in and out) on a mail server that isn't coming or going via TCP port 25.

Other clever filter tricks include "from" and "to" style commands where you can ignore entire directions of traffic at the touch of a key. These take the slightly more professional terminology of src and dst for *source* and *destination*.

One of my favorite parts of iftop's extensible configuration is the fact that you can mix and match almost every filter with other filters to get you the precision you require. Of course, mistakes (a typo or a missing dot to separate the octets of an IP address) happen, but generally I find the syntax of iftop is exceptionally intuitive.

Here are some more examples. You can conjure up a mix of hosts and ports with directional filters as follows:

```
dst host router.chrisbinnie.tld and src port bgpd and not host ntp.chrisbinnie.tld
```

Also, sometimes certain ranges of ports are useful. I can't help but think of ngrep and tcpdump again in relation to this next option.

The port numbers included in the following example are variously referred to as privileged ports, power ports, or special ports. They are referred to as such because, by default, on Linux systems only root can bind to these ports, leaving the upper level of ephemeral ports to non-superusers. The lowest 1024 TCP ports shown next can be checked as follows for suspicious traffic.

```
src host web.chrisbinnie.tld portrange 0-1024
```

You can also check for a specific protocol (a little like the ether option shown previously, but this time a transport protocol as opposed to a link type) using this:

```
ip proto name-of-protocol
```

To monitor a single subnet if your server can see multiple subnets, whether local or remote, use the following command:

```
# iftop -F 10.10.10.0/24
```

■ **Note** It's important to note that an uppercase *F* precedes a network option, as opposed to the lowercase version for enabling certain filtering.

Listening for Network Traffic

I once spent a great deal of time checking network anomalies only to discover that one subnet was effectively "bleeding" traffic over into another. The tool that lead me to this discovery was, of course, iftop. The following scenario will help explain what I'm talking about.

Like with some other packet sniffers and network monitors, you can (with superuser privileges) configure your network interface to drop into what is called "promiscuous" mode. iftop has the ability to listen for traffic travelling across the network port to which the interface is connected (whether that be a network switch, hub, or otherwise) but that isn't destined for the IP addresses bound to that interface. In other words, in some cases, you can pick and choose what to ignore from traffic that is not actually going to your server but is instead going via your network card. You can try to find out with the -p flag like this on the interface called eth0:

```
# iftop -p -i eth0
```

And, for personal preferences, the -B for viewing bytes rather than the network convention of bits (Kbps) can be added for ease:

```
# iftop -i eth0 -B
```

There are also a number of other display options that you might want to experiment with in order to change the screen to your preference. This switches off bar graphs (which I favor usually for clarity).

```
# iftop -b
```

Two other parameters that may come in handy, -P and -N:

- The uppercase -P option (not the same as *P* for freezing the display) ensures that all the ports involved in a network transaction (source and destination) will be visible in the display.

■ **Note** If higher-end port numbers don't have corresponding entries in the file /etc/services, then you'll just see the port number directly. Otherwise, you'll be presented with a port name such as www or domain for DNS, etc. Incidentally, I never turn this functionality off unless my display is brimming with information.

- The -N flag just reverses that option, thereby ignoring /etc/services entirely and the associated names, and purely concentrates on outputting raw port numbers only.

Changing Filters Can Take Time

Note that depending on your setup and circumstances, changing real-time filters may not yield immediate noticeable results. This is because like many measurements you're relying on averaging a number of results, albeit within a minuscule window usually, so you essentially have to wait for other parts of the display or network filter to catch up.

Configuring iftop Scenarios

Once you've cut your teeth on some of the more standard iftop config options, you might find yourself using it in a number of different scenarios. And, in, and around these scenarios if repetition creeps in then, as mentioned, it's useful to have a set configuration ready to use at the press of a key or two.

For example, you could have a bash alias or a simple script that references a few different config files held in the root user's home directory for iftop. Then you could trigger the pertinent config file by typing something akin to a shortcut for a config file along the lines of:

```
# iftop broadcast storm
```

The default config file referenced inside the home directories (usually root's because its system privileges are needed) is .iftoprc.

As promised, I wanted to walk through a few configuration options before passing on a fairly generic configuration file that you can add your own filters to; here goes:

```
# cat /root/.iftoprc

dns-resolution: yes
port-resolution: yes
show-bars: yes
promiscuous: yes
port-display: on
hide-source: no
hide-destination: no
use-bytes: no
sort: 2s
line-display: one-line-both
show-totals: yes
log-scale: yes
```

Many of these configuration options speak for themselves. The option line-display lets you combine the total traffic sum of inbound and outbound traffic to immediately show the busiest hosts in the display. This is instead of showing one output for inbound traffic and one for outbound. This config option can be changed in a number of ways: two-line, one-line-sent, one-line-received.

You may also want to add the "real" network capacity that you're connected to with the max-bandwidth option. Imagine for a moment that you are connected to a 1024Mbps network link (1Gbit), but your external Internet capacity is actually only 100Mbps (this could be your *committed data rate*). Sometimes your LAN might show you bursts of traffic that simply don't add up. In other words, you might see more than 100Mbps going out to the Internet, which simply can't be an accurate reflection of your traffic flows.

The excellent `iftop` lets you specify a bandwidth cap so that you can have a more realistic maximum is shown. One caveat; this needs to be in bits, not bytes:

```
max-bandwidth: 100M
```

Here, you can adjust the ceiling down to 100Mbps, even though you're using a gigabit LAN connection.

Using iftop on Busy Routers

I've successfully used `iftop` on very busy Linux routers (pushing hundreds of Mbit of traffic but more importantly with hundreds of thousands of concurrent network connections) and it stood up admirably time and time again. It's worth emphasizing this point because some other tools crashed the router under a decent level of load. `iftop` continues to serve honorably and remains stable even under high levels of stress. Of course, your mileage may vary, depending on versions and flavors, among other things, so try it in busy development environments first.

Should you try `iftop` on a busy router, it may not immediately occur to you that you will generate a massive amount of DNS lookups if that option is enabled. It can add a fairly noticeable load to a machine if it suddenly receives tens of thousands of tiny DNS packets, so initially for testing at the very least, and especially during busy spells, it's wise to disable them. You can use `-n` at startup to avoid your network interfaces panicking at the sudden, massive packets-per-second influx. It's an easy mistake to make and not one that I'd recommend accidentally doing on a production machine.

Summary

I trust this overview of the supercharged utility that is `iftop` has whet your appetite enough to fire it up and have a go at using it yourself. I have barely scratched the surface of the options available to you. The simple fact that this amazing utility complies with relatively complex filter changes while it's still running (at near real-time) makes it truly outstanding. However, coupled with the myriad of configurable options, suitable for almost all circumstances, it is undeniably a formidable network tool to be reckoned with. And what with the introduction of *regular expressions*, there genuinely is little that you can't observe on a network link with `iftop`. I hope you enjoy putting it through its paces as much as I frequently do.

CHAPTER 2

■ ■ ■

Destroying Sensitive Data

You may be familiar with popular Windows products like CCleaner; they clean up temporary files to help with privacy and as a result free up disk space. They also help declutter your registry from previously installed software. These actions are supposed to help improve the startup time of your computer after a reboot and improve performance overall. They also have specific profiles for certain applications, such as browsers, which allow them to target known spyware among other nefariously installed packages.

These products are undoubtedly useful tools that help with desktops, but have you ever thought about cleaning up drives on UNIX-type operating systems? Imagine, for example, that your boss asks you to track down a sensitive document that was copied across several servers by accident. He wants you to remove all copies of that document and quickly. The super-sensitive file is of such importance that you are even asked, in the event that one of the servers is stolen, to guarantee that none of the data can be recovered from any of its drives.

You could scrub the data off of, say, a whole disk partition to successfully destroy the said file, or even destroy all data on every drive attached to a server. Unfortunately, using the rm command is simply not enough to delete data properly. This is because the contents of the file still remain on the drive and the operating system simply ignores any reference to them. In this chapter, I cover three tools that you can use to destroy sensitive data selectively: shred, dd, and wipe. I also mention how to wipe entire disks by booting off external media or using DBAN.

A Note on Random Data Overwrites and Degaussing

When you attempt to wipe a drive or partition, the introduction of random data into the way you overwrite old data is important because of "data remnants". In essence there's a residual amount of data left even after the formatting of a drive.

As discussed, for performance reasons, operating systems generally prefer to ignore references to deleted files as opposed to actually removing their content. The idea behind the shred utility is to obfuscate contents by overwriting it with random data.

To be sure, some top-end laboratories can employ varying techniques to look past the obfuscation. In an effort to mitigate against these lab techniques, a few countermeasures have been innovated in the past. One such method is called the "Gutmann method," created by Peter Gutmann and Colin Plumb in 1996. Without getting too in-depth, it's debatable whether this approach is effective without knowing the innards of your drive relatively intimately. In brief, it appears to work by targeting three types of drive and particularly MFM and RLL encoded disks (http://redhill.net.au/d/10.php), which are now considered older, by writing 35 patterns over a disk to erase its data.

Sadly, this innovative method appears to be mostly deprecated thanks to the fact that it is no longer possible to predict how modern drives store their data. For more modern drives (PRML and EPRML drives—http://www.pcguide.com/ref/hdd/geom/dataEPRML-c.html), Gutmann said that scrubbing drives with random data is more effective as the encoding differs with MFM and RLL for which their technique was devised.

However, to help throw fuel on the fire, the National Institute of Standards and Technology (NIST) stated in 2006 that "most of today's media can be effectively cleared after one overwrite". To say that there's a lively, ongoing debate about the efficacy of varying data-destruction methods is an understatement.

Another method, called *degaussing*, is one that utilizes a degausser. These are usually specifically designed for a specific model of drive and procured at the time the drive is sourced.

Some degaussers are apparently fully trusted by the the National Security Agency (NSA) in the United States and can wipe very large storage media (including tapes) in as little 45 seconds. This method can make the media inoperable in the future and can be an expensive approach, although some manufacturers can sometimes restore a physical drive's functionality, albeit without the data, it seems.

Degaussing works by inserting a drive or tape into a huge, clumsy-looking, 1970s-style box device and then zapping it with large amounts of fluctuating magnetic energy. It effectively confuses the storage media's magnetic field to such a great extent it becomes neutralized. And, lo and behold, the drive's magnetic state is reset to nearly zero, and (in some cases) it can be treated as if it had just been freshly manufactured. One example of such a machine can be found at http://ep.yimg.com/ca/I/easycdduplication_2265_23575127.

Aside from clever, highly expensive hardware techniques, another common approach is to physically destroy the storage media. This somewhat Draconian approach includes dipping the salient components of the media (not the metal casing but just the components that hold the data) into specific chemicals. Alternatively, you can also use a grinding tool or simply set the media on fire.

■ **Note** For the following examples, I'll be using the Debian flavor of Linux, but your mileage shouldn't vary too much if you try out some of the examples on other flavors.

Using the shred Utility

When it comes to the destruction of data, one tool stands out from the crowd on UNIX-like systems: shred. This little binary lets you overwrite files if you need to hide their contents. Using shred, you can "just delete" files or, if necessary, overwrite a file repeatedly in order to help try and hide the file contents from even professional, mission-impossible hardware.

Note, as stated in the manual for the shred utility, that only certain filesystems are compatible with its modus operandi. It requires a filesystem that overwrites the data "in place" to work effectively. As stated in the manual, shred won't work as effectively on the following types of filesystems:

- Log-structured or journaled filesystems, such as those supplied with AIX and Solaris (and JFS, ReiserFS, XFS, Ext3, etc.)
- Filesystems that write redundant data and carry on even if some writes fail, such as RAID-based filesystems
- Filesystems that make snapshots, such as Network Appliance's NFS server
- Filesystems that cache in temporary locations, such as NFS version 3 clients
- Compressed filesystems

The long and short of it is that you can be pretty certain on filesystems other than those types listed that the shred utility has done its job admirably. Do not, however, bet the ranch on the results of any of the tools mentioned in this chapter, as computers sometimes do unexpected things. We've all experienced it.

Installing shred

Caveats aside, let's look at some of options the shred utility provides. The shred utility is part of the coreutils package, which should almost always be installed. As a result, if for some reason you can't run shred on Debian derivatives, then install it using this command:

```
# apt-get install coreutils
```

On Fedora and RHEL et al., you can try this:

```
# yum install coreutils
```

I'm sure you get the idea. Incidentally, it will be highly unusual not to have coreutils installed, owing to the fact that all your basic file, text, and shell utilities come with it. It's from whence ls and rm appear, for example.

Getting Started with shred

To get started, if you wanted to wipe an entire disk partition, you could begin as follows. This example targets the partition called sda3.

```
# shred -vfz -n 25 /dev/sda3
```

Here's how this command breaks down:

- The -f switch means that if the shred utility struggles with the requisite permissions needed to wipe a file or partition, you can simply "force" the operation to succeed. Be warned, though; it's frighteningly easy to lose precious data with this remarkable utility.

- The all-pervasive and friendly -v for displaying an operation's progress is commonplace and stands for *verbose*. To hide your tracks, you can add the -z or --zero switch, which adds an overwrite using zeros to cleverly disguise the act of shredding.

- Finally, -n 25 means that rather than the default three overwrites, you will hammer your disk 25 times to obfuscate the previously stored data. All very covert and professional.

This action also applies to RAID partitions. And, with the simplest of adjustments, if you wanted to wipe an entire drive then you'd just drop the partition number off the end. Very carefully try something along the following lines on a test box, with fewer overwrites for a big disk:

```
# shred -vfz -n 5 /dev/sdc
```

If privacy is your greatest concern, you can simply increase the overwrite settings. There's also another nice feature available in the shred utility. It lets you throw a file full of random data into the mix. You can achieve this by using this switch --random-source=*FILENAME*, where *FILENAME* refers to the name of your data file (although it doesn't have to be a data file; more on this shortly).

15

Using the dd Utility

An alternative to the shred utility is the well-known stalwart of the UNIX toolset: the dd utility. It is one of my favorite tools and can be used to copy data and unforgivingly destroy it (and it does so in an instant, so use it carefully!).

You can run a destructive dd utility command using the following parameters in this pseudocode:

```
# dd if=RANDOMDATA of=/dev/sda1 bs=<sector_size> count=<sector_number>
seek=<sector_where_to_start>
```

Here, the input data or file (if) is named RANDOMDATA (which I'll use as a variable for a random data source for now) and the "output file" (of) is an entire partition: /dev/sda1. The other parameters are yet to be populated and provide access to a number of options.

To find out the information required to fill in these fields, you run the fdisk command as the superuser, root; for example:

```
# fdisk -l /dev/sda1
```

Listing 2-1 shows the output of this command.

Listing 2-1. The Partition Information You Get for "/dev/sda1" When Running the "fdisk" Utility

```
Disk /dev/sda1: 524 MB, 524288000 bytes
64 heads, 32 sectors/track, 500 cylinders
Units = cylinders of 2048 * 512 = 1048576 bytes
Sector size (logical/physical): 512 bytes / 512 bytes
I/O size (minimum/optimal): 512 bytes / 512 bytes
Disk identifier: 0x00000000
```

Next, look at the disk size (524MB displayed in bytes) and the logical sectors associated with /dev/sda1, which are 512 bytes in this case.

To improve the performance of the dd command, you need to check the start sector of where your partition is. You do this by running fdisk on your whole drive (in modern versions of fdisk it's needed; older versions don't offer the output shown in Listing 2-1 quite as readily). Do it like this:

```
# fdisk -l /dev/sda
```

You get the following output:

```
Device Boot      Start        End     Blocks    Id   System
/dev/sda1    *       2        501     512000    83   Linux
/dev/sda2          502      19562    3120312    8e   Linux
```

Clearly, since it's easy to make mistakes and cause all sorts of damage to partitions when using this method, you may want to try these commands on a test machine first and look up the salient dd utility parameters very carefully indeed. Be sure to double-check partition names if you use them. As previously mentioned, the dd utility is truly fantastic (I used to mirror entire server drives in a data center back to servers in my office using dd, so I had replacement servers offsite), but there's little recourse if you mess up!

At this point, you have the information you need and can populate the destructive pseudo-command I mentioned earlier with real parameters:

```
# dd if=RANDOMDATA of=/dev/sda1 bs=512 count=501 seek=2
```

On any other partition, there would likely be a much larger "count". It's small here because it's a boot partition (probably initially loosely set at 512MB in case you're confused, even though it counts up to 524MB). The seek entry is also a small number because the partition starts at the beginning of the disk and is first in line as partition numero uno, and the bs is from the logical sector count. I haven't touched upon the if= setting for which I've only used RANDOMDATA. You may have already guessed that this setting might not necessarily be a file but instead you could indeed use /dev/zero or /dev/urandom. Both generate random data. Which of the two options is the most effective is up for debate, but counter-intuitively I would use /dev/zero if it were possible thanks to the fact it should use less CPU and might be a little faster.

Next, take a look at the following example:

```
# dd if=RANDOMDATA of=/dev/sda bs=<physical_sector> count=<every_physical_sector> seek=0
```

This example references /dev/sda (the whole drive) and starts a seek from 0. As a result, this command will wipe a whole drive. This example uses physical sectors, which you can get from the entry in this line (shown earlier in Listing 2-1):

```
Sector size (logical/physical): 512 bytes / 512 bytes
```

As you can see, it doesn't really matter whether you use logical or physical sectors in this case, as they're both "512 bytes" but that won't always be the case.

Finally, all you need under the count parameter is every_physical_sector on the drive and the good news is that the dd utility should work fine without requiring that number. The only thing that will happen is that the dd utility will probably display an error about writing data beyond known disk limits.

If you wanted to do things cleanly without errors, then you will need the size of the disk; in the following example, the size for /dev/sda is 24696061952 bytes.

```
Disk /dev/sda: 24.7 GB, 24696061952 bytes
64 heads, 32 sectors/track, 23552 cylinders
Units = cylinders of 2048 * 512 = 1048576 bytes
Sector size (logical/physical): 512 bytes / 512 bytes
I/O size (minimum/optimal): 512 bytes / 512 bytes
Disk identifier: 0x0008d52e
```

In order to work out the total number of physical sectors, you can use the following Bash sum on your command line:

```
# echo $((24696061952 / 512))
```

The first number is the total number of bytes on the drive and the second number relates to the sector size of physical sectors. Simply divide the big number by the smaller one and you get the number 48234496.

Using the wipe Utility

The wipe, or more accurately wipefs, command is a relative newcomer that is part of the util-linux-ng package. It enables you to remove a filesystem signature from a device, which in turn makes the filesystem non-existent according to libblkid (the block device identification library). The tool comes with an -a switch, which stands for "all partitions" and a -n switch, also known as --no-act option, which will run through what will be done without actually performing the final no-going-back write command.

The super-swift wipefs utility doesn't actually erase data from a device; it just obfuscates its existence to libblkid. For example, when you use "wipe" in combination with the fdisk utility (to check that you're referring to the correct drive), you can scrub an SD card or a USB stick very easily. First, you simply "unmount" the drive as follows:

```
# umount /dev/ARGH
```

Next, run the following command to wipe your whole drive's partition information (replacing ARGH with the correct drive name, such as sde for example):

```
# wipefs -a /dev/ARGH
```

The output is this:

```
/dev/sde: 2 bytes were erased at offset 0x000001fe (dos): 55 aa
/dev/sde: calling ioclt to re-read partition table: Success
```

Finally, when you run the following command, you'll see that the drive is gone:

```
# fdisk -l
```

Booting Off External Media

If you want to destroy *all* the data on *all* the drives of a server, you can wipe your root partition (which is otherwise in use by the operating system) by booting the system from an external boot media, such as Knoppix (http://www.knopper.net/knoppix/index-en.html), or you can check out testdisk (http://www.cgsecurity.org/wiki/TestDisk). In general, most distributions today have some live-boot capability on their boot media (USB sticks included). Use these with care if you're wiping whole drives.

DBAN

Along with an enterprise tool called *Blancco*, there's a tool named *DBAN*, which stands for Darik's Boot and Nuke (http://www.dban.org). DBAN targets the home-user market, but surprisingly it appears to meet six erasure standards. The enterprise version, Blancco, also seems like a pretty serious piece of software. It apparently includes compliance with more than 20 erasure standards. Blancco claims also to be approved by U.S. Department of Defense certification: DoD 5220.2M and NIST 800-88. In true enterprise standards, a shiny PDF or XML report can also be produced having executed a remapping of sectors, data-destroying run.

Summary

In this chapter, I explored ways to destroy data on a single partition and a whole drive. Additionally, by booting with external media, you can wipe every partition including the boot partition along with any drive connected to a server. Remember to take the utmost care when it comes to wiping data in large chunks of drives. Having a test server to try these commands on first definitely helps reduce the chance of causing irreparable damage to your precious data. Tread carefully when using these tools!

CHAPTER 3

■ ■ ■

Supercharged systemd

For a long time, the services handler called `init` was responsible for the initialization of services after a reboot. However, with each new release of Linux, `init` started to look more and more like an antique. One of the fundamental issues with `init` is that it runs in a linear fashion, which is hardly efficient when parallelization is possible. The chosen replacement after some debate was `systemd`. In this chapter, I run through how to interact with your `systemd` services and explore any pitfalls that you may encounter with the newer versions of Linux that use `systemd`.

Master the Basics

You will look at a few comparisons between the old and the new. The good news is that you can still launch services with commands such as `/etc/init.d/SERVICENAME start` should you need to.

However, the System Control binary that you need to get used to is referred to as `systemctl`. Going forward, commit the following to memory—the preferred start/stop "service" command format that you'll now need to use looks like this:

```
# systemctl start SERVICENAME.service
```

Note the new name `systemctl` at the start of that command and the optionally appended `.service` addition. Note also that you can swap out the word `start` with `restart`, `stop`, `reload`, and `status`, as you'd expect. Another option is `condrestart` (which also applies to `init`); `condrestart` will let you conditionally restart a service that is already running. Alternatively there are a few more characters added to the `systemd` command, as seen here:

```
# systemctl try-restart SERVICENAME.service
```

Additionally, you can try this handy old-school `service` command:

```
# service --status-all
```

This command runs through all of the "init scripts" sitting in the `/etc/init.d` directory and reports back whether they are started or stopped or, on a very basic level, might have issues. The `systemd` alternative in this case is:

```
# systemctl list-units --type service --all
```

And how do you set up your services to start and stop after a reboot? On Red Hat derivatives, you would probably use the `chkconfig` command. Let's look at Debian derivatives first, however.

Up until Debian 6.0, you might have used something like this command to start your service/daemon up at boot time:

```
# update-rc.d SERVICENAME defaults
```

On more recent Debian flavors, you were encouraged to use this command:

```
# insserv SERVICENAME
```

If you're still using the update-rc.d then you can run a no-op or dry-run check of the services in your /etc/init.d directory (without actually enabling them) by using:

```
# insserv n
```

And, to remove the service from firing up at boot time, this simple command will suffice:

```
# insserv r SERVICENAME
```

Before systemd, in order to get your scripts behaving throughout the varying run levels, it was important to write scripts that included an LSB (Linux Standard Base) header. These scripts might look something like the example in Listing 3-1, which shows an LSB header at the top of an init script (https://wiki.debian.org/LSBInitScripts, as created by the Debian Wiki team).

Listing 3-1. An LSB Header

```
### BEGIN INIT INFO
# Provides: scriptname
# Required-Start: $remote_fs $syslog
# Required-Stop: $remote_fs $syslog
# Default-Start: 2 3 4 5
# Default-Stop: 0 1 6
# Short-Description: Start daemon at boot time
# Description: Enable service provided by daemon.
### END INIT INFO
```

■ **Note** As a reminder of how things used to work, refer to https://wiki.debian.org/LSBInitScripts/DependencyBasedBoot.

To use systemd to start a particular service after a reboot, use this command:

```
# systemctl enable SERVICENAME.service
```

to switch it off, use this:

```
# systemctl disable SERVICENAME.service
```

Start at Boot

For the likes of Red Hat, Fedora, and CentOS distributions, which use the chkconfig command, the new systemd equivalents you can use are as follows. The command chkconfig SERVICENAME on simply becomes:

```
# systemctl enable SERVICENAME.service
```

In order to disable a service, you swap on and enable with disable and off, of course.

The familiar command that checks which run levels a service starts up on (chkconfig list SERVICENAME) can be swapped out with this command:

```
# systemctl status SERVICENAME.service
```

Incidentally, there are alternatives to some of these commands, and you can safely swap the word status out with is-enabled if you are so inclined. Also, to check whether services are running, you can use the option is-active instead. You may well be familiar with this command, which will show which services are set to do what and when:

```
# chkconfig --list
```

The now preferred command to look at all services and their startup settings is:

```
# systemctl list-unit-files --type service
```

Understand Units and Targets

Next we will consider the meaning of "units" when it comes to systemd. Units are really just config files of varying types that contain properties of a process that you want to manipulate.

Similarly, "targets" refer to a group of processes that you want to launch at the same time. They replace old-school run levels and are just a bunch of symlinks that point at your unit files. Don't worry about TARGETS though—they'll make more sense shortly—let's get back to units for now.

Units

You've already seen an example of a unit above: SERVICENAME.service. In systemd, units can include: automount, device, mount, path, service, socket, swap, snapshot, slice, scope, target, and timer.

You can explore the currently loaded units by using the following command (by the way, you can opt to use an equals sign after --type=):

```
# systemctl list-units --type service
```

Figure 3-1 shows the results of this command; as you can see, each unit comes with a useful level of detail. You can also ask to see "all" services with this (see Figure 3-1):

```
# systemctl list-units --all
```

You can experiment with these commands with relative impunity, but don't risk production systems until you're sure of what they do.

```
UNIT                            LOAD   ACTIVE SUB     DESCRIPTION
acpid.service                   loaded active running ACPI event daemon
apache2.service                 loaded active running LSB: Apache2 web server
console-kit-daemon.service      loaded active running Console Manager
console-kit-log-system-start.service loaded active exited  Console System Sta
console-setup.service           loaded active exited  LSB: Set console font and k
cron.service                    loaded active running Regular background program
dbus.service                    loaded active running D-Bus System Message Bus
fail2ban.service                loaded active running LSB: Start/stop fail2ban
getty@tty1.service              loaded active running Getty on tty1
hddtemp.service                 loaded active exited  LSB: disk temperature monit
ifup@eth0.service               loaded active exited  ifup for eth0
inetd.service                   loaded active running Internet superserver
irqbalance.service              loaded active exited  LSB: daemon to balance inte
kbd.service                     loaded active exited  LSB: Prepare console
keyboard-setup.service          loaded active exited  LSB: Set preliminary keymap
kmod-static-nodes.service       loaded active exited  Create list of required sta
mysql.service                   loaded active running LSB: Start and stop the mys
networking.service              loaded active exited  LSB: Raise network interfac
ntp.service                     loaded active running LSB: Start NTP daemon
postfix.service                 loaded active running LSB: Postfix Mail Transport
rc-local.service                loaded active exited  /etc/rc.local Compatibility
rsyslog.service                 loaded active running System Logging Service
ssh.service                     loaded active running OpenBSD Secure Shell server
systemd-journald.service        loaded active running Journal Service
systemd-logind.service          loaded active running Login Service
systemd-modules-load.service    loaded active exited  Load Kernel Modules
systemd-random-seed.service     loaded active exited  Load/Save Random Seed
systemd-remount-fs.service      loaded active exited  Remount Root and Kernel Fil
systemd-setup-dgram-qlen.service loaded active exited  Increase datagram queu
systemd-sysctl.service          loaded active exited  Apply Kernel Variables
systemd-tmpfiles-setup-dev.service loaded active exited  Create Static Device
systemd-tmpfiles-setup.service  loaded active exited  Create Volatile Files an
systemd-udev-trigger.service    loaded active exited  udev Coldplug all Devices
systemd-udevd.service           loaded active running udev Kernel Device Manager
systemd-update-utmp.service     loaded active exited  Update UTMP about System Bo
systemd-user-sessions.service   loaded active exited  Permit User Sessions
udev-finish.service             loaded active exited  Copy rules generated while
user@1000.service               loaded active running User Manager for UID 1000

LOAD   = Reflects whether the unit definition was properly loaded.
ACTIVE = The high-level unit activation state, i.e. generalization of SUB.
SUB    = The low-level unit activation state, values depend on unit type.

38 loaded units listed. Pass --all to see loaded but inactive units, too.
To show all installed unit files use 'systemctl list-unit-files'.
```

Figure 3-1. *The output displayed when requesting a list of the currently-loaded service "units"*

Should you want to see all services and units loaded, not just those running, run this command instead:

```
# systemctl list-units --all
```

Targets

There is no longer any concept of run levels with systemd. Instead use "targets," which simply point at lots of units so that you can launch them all together. To see all the targets on your system, you can use this command:

```
# systemctl list-unit-files --type=target
```

If you get caught with the new commands, remember that commands like /etc/init.d/SERVICENAME start and service SERVICENAME start do (distro-dependent possibly) still have some effect, so don't be too concerned if you're in a hurry.

To help me learn, I opted to create a few different Bash aliases to keep me right. If you like, you can also add comments about the commands in your ~/.bashrc file alongside your Bash aliases. You can then look at your user's and the "root" user's Bash history whenever you need to run commands, eventually committing them to memory.

If you wanted to view the default target that triggers all the unit files under its dependency tree, then you can use this command:

```
# systemctl get-default
```

Table 3-1 shows how the standard targets work in relation to old-school run levels, some of which include Graphical User Interfaces (GUIs).

Table 3-1. *Old-School Run Levels Versus New systemd Targets*

Run Level	Systemd Targets	Function
0	runlevel0.target, poweroff.target	Shut down and power off
1	runlevel1.target, rescue.target	Launch a rescue shell
2	runlevel2.target, multi-user.target	Launch a non-GUI, multi-user system
3	runlevel3.target, multi-user.target	Launch a non-GUI, multi-user system
4	runlevel4.target, multi-user.target	Launch a non-GUI, multi-user system
5	runlevel5.target, graphical.target	Launch a GUI, multi-user system
6	runlevel6.target, reboot.target	Shut down and reboot

As mentioned previously, the reason for having these target units is to pull together systemd units and their associated dependencies. The GNOME Windows Manager (gdm.service) would trigger the multi-user.target target, for example. And, in return, the multi-user.target Target starts any required or essential services. In addition, a target called basic.target gets fired.

Similar to init, systemd also uses symlinks. If you wanted to change the system's run level, for example, you would delete the existing run level like this:

```
# rm /etc/systemd/system/default.target
```

And to launch your GUI run level, you would then create a new symlink like this:

```
# ln -sf /lib/systemd/system/graphical.target /etc/systemd/system/default.target
```

The multi-user (run level 5) symlink could be found here /lib/systemd/system/multi-user.target too, for example. Without a reboot, you can change targets immediately within the current session as follows:

```
# systemctl isolate TARGETNAME.target
```

In other words, if you wanted to switch off your GUI and immediately change into multi-user mode, then this command would allow you to do that:

```
# systemctl isolate multiuser.target
```

If you wanted to change run levels in the past, then you would essentially start all "units" that are associated with a particular target and then dutifully stop any that are no longer needed.

The rescue mode included with systemd is similar to Windows Safe Mode:

```
# systemctl rescue
```

Rescue mode will try to mount all the listed drives but leave your box off the network (avoiding logins from other users as a result). You will need the superuser password to execute this command and you might think of this mode as the equivalent of single-user mode. You will also alarmingly broadcast a warning, about the change in system state to all other users logged onto the system, and potentially drop lots of traffic to your box. Use this short command with caution.

There's also emergency mode, which means that you mount your "root" filesystem as read-only and don't mount your other drives. For an active production system, such an action can be seriously devastating in terms of your users losing data and access. Drop into that mode like this (with care):

```
# systemctl emergency
```

The emergency target only uses these dependencies:

```
emergency.service
```
- ├─.mount
- └─system.slice

For a comparison of the many dependencies that the multi-user target looks after, try running:

```
# systemctl list-dependencies multi-user.target
```

Explore the Analysis Tool

A nice addition to systemd is an analysis tool. Using it, you can appreciate the performance improvements over init. You can run it like this:

```
# systemd-analyze
Startup finished in 1258ms (kernel) + 1132ms (initramfs) + 111111ms (userspace) = 113501ms
```

As you can see, this clever little tool dutifully reports how quickly your systemd machine is booting up.

You can also add a few options to perform further analysis on your boot performance. Here is an interesting option:

```
# systemd-analyze blame
```

As shown in Figure 3-2, the blame option produces a list of those services that are slowing down your power-up times. A co-located server I have only apparently struggles when launching my database service, "mysql" for example. Even Apache is lightning fast, taking a little over a second, as is my mail server, the postfix.service.

```
11.078s mysql.service
 2.252s console-kit-log-system-start.service
 2.248s systemd-logind.service
 2.242s rc-local.service
 2.241s ntp.service
 2.240s keyboard-setup.service
 2.239s irqbalance.service
 2.239s hddtemp.service
 1.987s networking.service
 1.473s rsyslog.service
 1.111s apache2.service
 1.063s postfix.service
  671ms systemd-setup-dgram-qlen.service
  671ms sys-kernel-debug.mount
  670ms dev-hugepages.mount
  670ms dev-mqueue.mount
  487ms systemd-udev-trigger.service
  449ms kbd.service
  378ms systemd-tmpfiles-setup.service
  331ms fail2ban.service
  324ms kmod-static-nodes.service
  288ms systemd-tmpfiles-setup-dev.service
  248ms systemd-remount-fs.service
  216ms systemd-modules-load.service
  204ms systemd-sysctl.service
  180ms systemd-user-sessions.service
  178ms console-kit-daemon.service
  178ms udev-finish.service
  130ms systemd-random-seed.service
  110ms console-setup.service
   69ms dev-disk-by\x2duuid-6f8a4a9f\x2d264d\x2d4e41
   36ms systemd-udevd.service
   35ms systemd-update-utmp.service
   10ms user@1000.service
    5ms systemd-journal-flush.service
    4ms systemd-tmpfiles-clean.service
    3ms systemd-update-utmp-runlevel.service
```

Figure 3-2. *Who is to blame for a slow boot time? Use the "blame" option*

I briefly mentioned the dependency issues associated with init. If you are checking your boot times, then try the following option in order to display what is happening to the systemd units during your boot process:

```
# systemd-analyze critical-chain
```

```
The time after the unit is active or started is printed after the "@" charact
The time the unit takes to start is printed after the "+" character.

graphical.target @18.629s
└─multi-user.target @18.629s
  └─postfix.service @17.565s +1.063s
    └─mysql.service @6.486s +11.078s
      └─basic.target @6.473s
        └─paths.target @6.473s
          └─acpid.path @6.473s
            └─sysinit.target @6.460s
              └─networking.service @4.471s +1.987s
                └─systemd-random-seed.service @4.340s +130ms
                  └─systemd-remount-fs.service @4.091s +248ms
                    └─keyboard-setup.service @1.849s +2.240s
                      └─systemd-udevd.service @1.812s +36ms
                        └─systemd-tmpfiles-setup-dev.service @1.523s +288ms
                          └─kmod-static-nodes.service @1.198s +324ms
                            └─system.slice @1.158s
                              └─-.slice @1.158s
```

Figure 3-3. *There's lots of useful output from the "critical-chain" option*

You can even create SVG files (XML-based "Scalable Vector Graphic" files), which are graphical files, useful for visualizing information.

```
# systemd-analyze plot > steffi_graf.svg
```

This command will create a useful horizontal bar graph that proficiently illustrates the full timeline of your boot process, including when things are launched and those that run in parallel. If you're struggling with boot times and want to improve your machine's boot performance, then experiment with the plotting of these graphs.

There's a comprehensive web page from a Linux distribution called "OpenMadriva Lx" with an SVG graph as an example. It can be found under the section "7.26.3—Analyze the boot systemd-analyze" at https://doc.openmandriva.org/OpenMandriva-Lx-2014.

Power Options

Let's look at some simple tasks. For example, instead of shutdown -h now, you can use this command:

```
# systemctl poweroff
```

A reboot is easy to initiate:

```
# systemctl reboot
```

Similarly an old-style pm-suspend can use power management to suspend the system like this:

```
# systemctl suspend
```

To hibernate your machine, try this command:

```
# systemctl hibernate
```

To hibernate and suspend your system at the same time, use this:

```
# systemctl hybrid-sleep
```

Checking the Logs

When you need to check the systemd logs, you rely on journald. The powerful systemd introduces its own new logging system. From the oldest entry first, you can check all log entries quite easily. My Bash alias for this function is simply:

```
alias jj='journalctl'
```

The command in question, as shown in my alias, is:

```
# journalctl
```

You can also save data from old reboots. Apparently some Linux distributions enable this as standard but it seems that some do not. Have a look in the config file /etc/systemd/journald.conf to alter this behavior. You probably need to change the current line to make data storage "persistent" under the [Journal] section to enable it:

```
Storage=persistent
```

For all the kernel messages from systemd (similar to dmesg), you simply run this command:

```
# journalctl -k -b
```

The -b switch means just pay attention to this last boot; remove -k as required.
A simple Unix-type commands is:

```
# who -b
```

This command outputs the date and time of the last reboot. Another way of finding out that information is:

```
# last | less
```

systemd also has its own command:

```
# journalctl --list-boots
```

The output gives a simple list of past reboots with reference numbers in the left-side column that you can use to select specific instances from. Look here, where -1 is the boot-number reference:

```
# journalctl -b -1
```

Another logging feature is the time frames from within which you can query. For example, this command doesn't need much explanation:

```
# journalctl --since yesterday
```

You might want to try querying a specific service like dbus, for example, using this powerful command:

```
# systemctl status -l dbus.service
```

It will offer you logging and service status.
There are more options. This powerful example hopefully speaks for itself:

```
# journalctl --since="2011-11-11 11:11:11" --until "1 hour ago"
```

What about trimming that command down to reflect the last 15 minutes? You can use this format too:

```
# journalctl --since "15 min ago"
```

You can also "follow" the log, with -f just like the tail -f command, and additionally view the last 500 lines as so, with this command:

```
# journalctl -fan500
```

These are all powerful additions to your systemd toolkit to help diagnose issues. If you look once again in the config file /etc/systemd/journald.conf, you will see that you can also adjust a number of the logger's settings with relative ease. You'll see one simple example, but there are many: SystemMaxUse=.
This option reflects the most disk space that can be used for persistent storage.

Mind the Syntax

Next, let's explore an extension to what you've learned so far. It's important to make sure that your logs are how you want them to be. If you need to check the time configuration of your systemd logger then you can use this command:

```
# timedatectl status
```

You should then be informed of useful things such as whether NTP (Network Time Protocol) time syncing is enabled and which timezone the systemd config expects to be accurate with this command:

```
# timedatectl list-timezones
```

You would then pick a zone and set it using your preference instead of ZONENAME like this:

```
# timedatectl set-timezone ZONENAME
```

Init Scripts

The creation of custom init scripts is frequently necessary. Not all applications, even those sold to enterprises on UNIX-type systems, come with their own init scripts. It is therefore important to be able to write your own if necessary. Consider as an example that you may need to ignore a legacy installation and use an init script to dynamically work out which application to launch. This task needs to be done on hundreds of servers. It might be easier simply to drop a replacement init script into place than to add unnecessary risk by removing production applications.

Here are a few simple examples of how to write custom systemd startup scripts. Listing 3-2 shows an example service called chrisbinnie-cleanup.

Listing 3-2. A Very Simple systemd Startup Script

```
[Unit]
Description=Clear out an old disk cache somewhere
[Service]
Type=oneshot
ExecStart=/usr/sbin/chrisbinnie-cleanup
[Install]
WantedBy=multi-user.target
```

As you can see, this example declares a service. The line showing Type=oneshot is present because you just want this unit to execute an action but without continuing to run processes afterward (remember the "daemonize" terminology from init). You might consider using this example for clearing a disk cache; the script's task is over once it has run and only applicable as a one-time operation.

To enable it for startup at boot time, run this command:

```
# systemctl enable chrisbinnie
```

Consider the scenario where you might only want to start a daemon once. That is the case even though it will be requested as a dependency by many different services. The "oneshot" option applies here, but you could achieve that functionality by using the RemainAfterExit=yes option, as shown in Listing 3-3.

Listing 3-3. A Oneshot and Remain Example

```
[Unit]
Description=Simple Oneshot And Remain Scenario
[Service]
Type=oneshot
RemainAfterExit=yes
ExecStart=/usr/local/bin/save-oldest-config
ExecStop=/usr/local/bin/save-ferris
[Install]
WantedBy=multi-user.target
```

In Listing 3-3, systemd knows that the script started successfully and will therefore treat it as remaining "active". Running the script again won't trigger any actions as a result.

Another simple example would be a script that integrates with systemd and sends a notification about how successful its launch was, as shown in Listing 3-4.

Listing 3-4. This Useful "notify" Option as Shown Inside a Service File

```
[Unit]
Description=Notify next of kin
[Service]
Type=notify
ExecStart=/usr/sbin/notifying-next-of-kin-service
[Install]
WantedBy=multiuser.target
```

You should be aware that the service has to be able to inform systemd of its successful startup. Otherwise, it will treat it as having failed and therefore kill it off after a timeout period. There is more on this subject in the manual here (possibly distro-dependent):

```
# man sd_notify
```

As you can imagine, there are a number of other options to consider here, but hopefully you understand the basics now. Table 3-2 lists some other options to ruminate over (the manual includes several others).

Table 3-2. Other Useful Commands to Start and Stop Services

Command	Action
ExecStartPre	Run me before ExecStart
ExecStopPost	Run me after ExecStop
ExecStartPost	Run me after my ExecStart commands have finished
ExecStopPost	Run me after ExecStop
RestartSec	Sleep time before restarting my service
ExecReload	Run me when a reload is requested
ExecStart	Core commands to run
ExecStop	If the unit has failed or it is stopped manually

Migrating to Systemd

For a reassuring conversation about how a lengthy, cumbersome init script can be converted from the old into the new, refer to http://serverfault.com/questions/690155/whats-the-easiest-way-to-make-my-old-init-script-work-in-systemd. Note in particular that the line beginning with ExecStart contains your standard launch parameters.

The conversation shown on that page might be one that you will be having with other sysadmins for a few years to come.

Summary

systemd introduces a major architectural change for Linux. With its day-to-day use, I can see both benefits and frustrations ahead. Whatever your preference, you need to learn its basic concepts and its simple command-line functionality even if it is discontinued in the future.

CHAPTER 4

■ ■ ■

Zero Downtime Linux

One of the key factors that made me take Unix-type systems so seriously, when compared to Microsoft servers, was the lack of reboots that were required for production systems.

In my experience, after their initial build you can generally expect Unix derivatives to run continuously for a year without even a hint of them needing your attention. Some sysadmins even claim to have inherited boxes that haven't been rebooted for a decade and, in the right environment, I can believe it. That's not to encourage such a practice, of course, because that means there hasn't been any kernel security patching taking place over that decade.

As some of you know, a few years ago that last statement became obsolete. That's because for a relatively short period of time, sysadmins have been able to patch their Linux kernels live and without any disruption to services or reboots. In this chapter, I discuss how the year 2015 advanced live kernel patching on Linux one important step further. The chapter also explores some of the immediately available options to those wanting to take advantage of this illuminating technology. Those sysadmins who do are certain to benefit from a significant increase in uptime and security on their production servers.

Incidentally, when it comes to monitoring, you can keep a much closer eye on your reboots (accidental or otherwise) and overall uptime by using a clever little tool called `tuptime`, which can be found at `https://github.com/rfrail3/tuptime`.

The Promise of Continuous Availability

I should say that I've long been a proponent that critical services should not aim for high availability (HA) but instead continuous availability (CA). I remember reading that the massive online video streaming giant, Netflix (`http://www.netflix.com`), conceded that even they had to accept their service would fail at certain points despite the unquestionable might of the cloud technologies that they employed. It's quite a remarkable statement if you think about it; assuming that Netflix has some of the best architects and engineers on the planet working for it and reportedly now uses the dominant cloud provider, Amazon Web Services, almost exclusively.

Over the last few years, I've been following with interest the attempts by developers to provide solutions to the live patching of kernels. As mentioned, such a solution removes the need to reboot a Linux server after applying a kernel patch; these patches might fix security headaches or apply well-needed bug fixes.

As a result of my interest in this area, when the first fully-matured commercial service came to market, I became one of the earlier customers of Ksplice's "Uptrack" service (`http://www.ksplice.com`). This was at the start of 2010. Even at that stage I found the service to be very slick and used it around-the-clock for years on key production servers, predominantly running Debbie and Ian's favorite distribution of Linux. I'll cover Uptrack in a little more depth later on.

The main aim of Uptrack (for my purposes at least) was to defer reboots and keep the number of maintenance windows, which had to start at midnight, to an absolute minimum. These were mostly only required following the application of kernel security patches. Such a patching run might be required from three times a year to once a month, depending on what you were using your machines for and the versions or bugs involved.

Ksplice's Uptrack (then just referred to as "Ksplice" from what I can gather) was mainly authored by an unquestionably clever man called Jeff Arnold at the Massachusetts Institute of Technology. Even during its testing phase, where 50 kernel vulnerabilities from May 2005 to December 2007 were studied, Ksplice was able to successfully patch an impressive 84% of those presented.

It's safe to say that Ksplice was the first notable commercial enterprise that attracted attention in the marketplace. Nowadays, there are also other conspicuous competitors such as KernelCare (http://www.kernelcare.com), which, at the time of writing, has around 2,500 providers using its software service according to its web site.

As with all exciting new technologies, a degree of landscape change is inevitable. Oracle acquired Ksplice in July, 2011 and as a result the service is now only offered to Oracle Linux Premier Support customers. Legacy customers (I'm very pleased to say) are still able to use their accounts.

Two quotes that caught my attention a while ago were made by the venerable Linus Torvalds when kernel version 4 went live on April 12, 2015. There was much ado in the press about the jump to version 4 of the kernel, mainly because of the sizeable jump in version numbers I suspect (see Figure 4-1). Good, old Torvalds, who at times can be a master of the understatement, said that the new kernel "doesn't have all that much special" and that "much have been made of the new kernel patching infrastructure". He cited the main reason of the version bump being because lots of housekeeping was done.

mainline:	**4.2**	2015-08-30
stable:	**4.1.6**	2015-08-17
longterm:	**3.18.21**	2015-08-31
longterm:	**3.14.51**	2015-08-17
longterm:	**3.12.47**	2015-08-27
longterm:	**3.10.87**	2015-08-17
longterm:	**3.4.108**	2015-06-19
longterm:	**3.2.71**	2015-08-12
longterm:	**2.6.32.67**	2015-06-03
linux-next:	**next-20150910**	2015-09-10

Figure 4-1. *There was a big jump in kernel version numbers this year*

I suspect that quote about the kernel patching was a case of everyone talking about something "new" to such an extent that in his mind it quickly became "old" news. Far be it from me to argue with anyone like Torvalds and his deity-like status; I'm sure that he wouldn't mind me saying that the newer kernels do include the most important change to live kernel patching for some time.

Live Patching the Kernel

The fact that live kernel patching code now sits inside the mainstream kernel, known as `livepatch`, was a contentious topic for a while, albeit only the foundations of the code that will ultimately be required.

The story goes that long-standing Linux stalwart, SUSE (https://www.suse.com/products/live-patching/), harking back to 1992, was developing "kGraft" in order to provide zero downtime functionality for their enterprise customers running SUSE Enterprise Linux. Meanwhile, Red Hat was developing kPatch (http://rhelblog.redhat.com/2014/02/26/kpatch/), which is now included in Red Hat Enterprise Linux (RHEL) version 7.0 as a "technology preview".

It seems that the sometimes vociferous Torvalds had something to say about two solutions that essentially solve the same problem being present in the Linux kernel: "It pretty quickly became obvious to the interested parties that it's absolutely impractical in this case to have several isolated solutions for one task to coexist in the kernel."

When debates were taking place about whether the kernel would include kGraft or kPatch, it appeared that Red Hat did have a slight advantage. This was thanks to the fact that there was no advanced preparation required for the kernel in order to allow a system to use live kernel updates and that errors were caught better.

After lots of humming and harring, an agreement was reached. The long and short of such a discussion (http://linuxplumbersconf.org/2014/wp-content/uploads/2014/10/LPC2014_LivePatching.txt) can be summed up as follows: "Question: Can we run both kPatch and kGraft in same kernel? Answer: Yes!"

There was then apparently a new kernel patch written by Red Hat called `livepatch` that enabled both kGraft and kPatch to operate in perfect harmony. Having had it reviewed in November 2014, the code was accepted as being able to cut the mustard and dutifully merged into the kernel by Torvalds et al. in February 2015.

It's been said that neither Red Hat nor SUSE were (officially at least) aware of each other's project to provide live kernel patching. What matters is that a fair compromise was reached and both parties have been left feeling satisfied, publically at least.

According to the code commit that Torvalds submitted to the kernel, Red Hat's kPatch works by sending the kernel a `stop_machine()` when it is satisfied that it is safe to do so. At that point, it injects the new code into the live kernel. Don't get me wrong, we're not forcing a "halt" or anything that lasts more than a fraction of a second, so it's effectively an instantaneous action that your server doesn't even notice.

Apparently kGraft, on the other hand, works on a per-task basis by keeping track of checkpoints, achieving its goals by patching as it goes. There's a sample of the ruminations that were involved in a post by someone who knows their stuff from SUSE at https://lkml.org/lkml/2014/11/7/354.

As a result of compromises, relatively minor rewrites and a healthy dose of cooperation, you now have the basic infrastructure required for live kernel patching present in Linux. This includes an application programming interface (API) and an application binary interface (ABI), which allow userspace to enable, disable, and display a list of which patches were applied. It's certainly a good start.

Apparently, the live kernel patching software makes great use of the kernel's `ftrace` ("function tracer") functionality. The code is entirely self-contained, which means that it doesn't even speak to other components of the kernel or more accurately cause them any undue disruption. At the time of release, only x86 hardware was able to take advantage of the technology. PowerPC, S/390, and ARM are already being looked at for its inclusion in their kernels.

Torvalds notes that "once this common infrastructure gets merged, both Red Hat and SUSE have agreed to immediately start porting their current solutions on top of this, abandoning their out-of-tree code." To get to this stage, both parties took their respective development paths relatively seriously, which in turn is promising for ongoing development. One example is that, in 2014, Red Hat started a Special Interest Group (SIG) for its existing customers using their RHEL 7 servers. As multiple common vulnerabilities and exposures (CVEs) were announced a few CVEs were handpicked and offered to users to see how easy it was to live patch against security issues and bug fixes.

Ksplice's Uptrack

Figure 4-2 shows the modus operandi behind live kernel patching, as demonstrated by Oracle's Ksplice service called "Uptrack". The uname -r command lets you display the --kernel-release in use by the system.

```
(root) # uname -r
2.6.39-300.26.1.el6uek.x86_64
(root) # uptrack-upgrade -y
Installing [guclwyc2] CVE-2012-0957: Information leak in uname syscall.
Installing [j4d07e02] Kernel panic in IPv4 ARP and IPv6 Neighbor Discovery.
Installing [r8og1ec4] CVE-2013-1979: Privilege escalation with UNIX socket credentials.
Installing [fiq04xbb] CVE-2013-2237: Information leak on IPSec key socket.
Installing [9q4luou3] CVE-2014-3687: Remote denial-of-service in SCTP stack.
Your kernel is fully up to date.
Effective kernel version is 2.6.39-400.215.13.el6uek
(root) # uptrack-uname -r
2.6.39-400.215.13.el6uek.x86_64
(root) #
```

Figure 4-2. *Oracle Ksplice's magical Upstart in a nutshell, displayed at* http://ksplice.oracle.com

Running the uptrack-upgrade command with the -y option ("yes") installs all of the available patches being offered at that time by Uptrack.

Finally, when running uptrack-uname -r, you are able check the effective kernel release in use by the system (note -400 versus -300). It all happens in an instant. Isn't that clever? You can certainly see why Red Hat and SUSE got in on the act after Uptrack hit the market.

Next, to check which patches have been applied by Uptrack, you can run the following command:

```
# uptrack-show
```

If you manually installed a few patches but have missed some, or if you want to see which have yet to be applied, you can try this command:

```
# uptrack-show --available
```

You can also set up fully automatic patching by changing the relevant line in the config file /etc/uptrack/uptrack.conf. I'd recommend avoiding this for production boxes and suggest that you only use this feature on less critical systems until you've tested the patches for obvious reasons. You could use something like Puppet to trigger the upgrade command around your server estate. Once you've tested the patches on a box, with the same kernel version and distribution, the rest of the estate would then patch themselves automatically.

Also within that config file, you can set install_on_reboot so that following a (potentially unexpected) reboot the patches will be bumped up to the same level as before without needing to hurriedly apply your kernel updates through your package manager. If there are other updates that could have also have been applied, then you probably want to set the option upgrade_on_reboot to "yes" to incorporate those too.

If you ever need to remove patches, then simply use this command in order to remove them all:

```
# uptrack-remove -y
```

Alternatively, rather than -y you can choose specifically which patch to remove by using a Ksplice ID (which you can glean from the uptrack-show command). You might need to use this if there's ever a patch misbehaving with, for example, a driver for some of your system hardware.

First Impressions

I can say with all honesty that during the years I used Uptrack on mission-critical Linux routers, I didn't suffer any unwelcome downtime and found the service from Ksplice to be excellent. Note though that the key word is "service".

The premise of live kernel patching (for all intents and purposes) is taking a diff to compare what was and what is "different" in the current kernel. Programmers then meticulously pick through the bones of the patch to be applied and create a specific type of patch that can be deployed in their patching infrastructure. This is then replicated (sometimes using different specialist kernel programmers) across the different architectures and distributions that they supported.

Back in the day, prior to the acquisition by Oracle, which understandably locked it down somewhat for use by its premium customers, there were many more distributions supported by Ksplice. That said, RHEL, CentOS, Debian, Ubuntu, Virtuozzo, and OpenVZ patches are still available to previous customers—for now at least. If my memory serves, I used Ksplice in production without any headaches on early container technology (which is still excellent incidentally), namely OpenVZ.

If you're interested in trying out the magic yourself, however, Ubuntu and Fedora users can install a free desktop edition. I'd highly recommend it; the desktop page can be found at http://www.ksplice.com/try/desktop.

The only issues that I encountered (and Ksplice staff at the time responded quickly) occurred on two separate occasions. This was when seemingly harmless error messages were generated following the application of some kernel patches. Needless to say, if I'm logged into a production system and I see nasty-looking errors that certainly shouldn't be there, I'm on the case immediately. The support team was clearly very able and prompt to respond despite, being in a different timezone (and despite the fact that I was only a few-dollars-a-month customer). Otherwise, the most important factor, that of course being the reliability of my very precious production systems, was flawless. This meant that I managed to sleep for many hours more when I would have otherwise been awake squinting at screens during a number of different maintenance windows.

KernelCare—Worth the Cost

I would be remiss not to mention KernelCare's offering in a little more detail. Now that Ksplice is essentially an exclusive club, there's little stopping you going to KernelCare. It is a service run by a company called CloudLinux, which has been around since 2009 and aims to make sysadmins' lives as easy as possible. The fact that Ksplice began offering CloudLinux as one of its supported distros in August 2010 (https://www.cloudlinux.com/company/news/index.php?ELEMENT_ID=495), prior to the Oracle acquisition, has not escaped me.

If you're using KernelCare's service for two machines and more, it's less than three dollars each month per machine. Believe me when I say that when your key engineers walk into work looking well-rested for several months in a row, those few dollars are well worth it. I haven't tried the KernelCare service myself, but it's safe to say that trying it out for a few months on less critical systems is a good way of dipping your toe in the water.

The nice thing about the live kernel patching business model is that, because of the number of supported distributions and architectures being so relatively few, if the service provider's programmers mess up porting a patch to their service then all hell breaks loose. Hundreds if not thousands of customers will be affected, which generally means a pretty swift fix if a failure occurs and lots of decent testing beforehand.

KernelCare certainly appears to have ambitions to pick up where Ksplice left off. A quote from the web site follows and bear in mind that there's a very low entry point, allowing just one server a month to use its service for a few dollars: "KernelCare supports CentOS/RHEL 5, 6 and 7, CloudLinux 5 and 6, OpenVZ, Virtuozzo, PCS, Debian 6 and 7 and Ubuntu 14.04. Other kernels will follow." There's also a mailing list to keep abreast of developments: `http://kernelcare.com/mailing-lists.php`.

One thing I remember that might be worth pointing out is that, using Uptrack at least, even if you are automatically applying your kernel patches, you should bear in mind that you're not also, by default, applying updates to your operating system's Uptrack package. In short, join the mailing list to make sure you know when important changes are made to the software; this applies to the patches too.

Try kPatch

Rather than trying out a commercial service, thanks to the new mainstream kernel code from Red Hat and SUSE, you can actually get your hands dirty immediately if you want. Be aware that it's still in the early days, however. One example is by visiting this kPatch page on the excellent GitHub: `https://github.com/dynup/kpatch`.

It's pretty difficult to miss the caveat in rather large letters near the top of that page, and I'd take this advice if I were you:

> "WARNING: Use with caution! Kernel crashes, spontaneous reboots, and data loss may occur!"

There's also a useful and brief explanation of this kPatch method and `livepatch`:

> "Starting with Linux 4.0, the Linux kernel has livepatch, which is a new converged live kernel patching framework. Livepatch is similar in functionality to the kpatch core module, though it doesn't yet have all the features that kpatch does."

Fedora 21, RHEL 7, CentOS 7, Oracle Linux 7, Ubuntu 14.04, Debian 8, and Debian 7.x are mentioned as prerequisites at the time of writing. The next caveat however mentions that "the `kpatch-build` command has only been tested and confirmed to work on Fedora 20, RHEL 7, Oracle Linux 7, CentOS 7, and Ubuntu 14.04" even though modern kernels should support it fine.

There's also a nicely written "How It Works" section, the mechanism's limitations, and a relatively comprehensive FAQ with some decent technical detail for those interested. I'll be keeping a close eye on that page over the coming months to see how things progress.

Not the End of Reboots

Live kernel patching technology certainly does not mean the end of reboots as we know it.

I tried to do some reading up on this subject a few years ago, having become intrigued with the `lsof` command's functionality present in the Debian command `checkrestart` (which is buried inside the `debian-goodies` package if you're interested). The invaluable `checkrestart` essentially looks for old files that are still in use after a new file has replaced it on the filesystem.

It checks for files being kept open by processes and then compares the list with those files still actually visible on your filesystem. After that, it dutifully warns if non-existent "old" files are still loaded in memory (they could pose a security risk for example).

It's certainly not uncommon for these culprits to be shared libraries. Once it has identified which services need "refreshed" then the clever `checkrestart` offers a few suggestions on how to do just that with init script formats, such as `service postfix restart` or `/etc/init.d/postfix restart`.

The latest version of the Debian distro, code-named "Jessie," has a new `systemd`-friendly incarnation called `needrestart`. I like the fact that `needrestart` is presented in a package of its own, as it will probably get more coverage and be developed further if it's popular. It's no longer buried deep inside a goody bag.

Some of the features of `needrestart`—the newer version of `checkrestart` that's bundled with "Jessie"—include (per `https://packages.debian.org/jessie/admin/needrestart`):

- Support for `systemd` (but does not require it)

- Binary blacklisting (i.e. display managers)

- Detection of pending kernel upgrades

- Detection of required restarts of interpreter-based daemons

- Support for Perl, Python, and Ruby

- Full integration into the `apt`/`dpkg` using hooks

If you run these tools (or the `lsof` command on its own) then some services such as `glibc` and `dbus` will likely show lots of results after certain upgrades. You soon realize (I think that it's a great learning experience) that after some package upgrades, it's almost impossible not to knock the server over when clearing down the multitudinous shared libraries manually.

As a result, until there's a consensus to absolutely ensure that every package and service can "live restart" without bringing a server down, then unfortunately production server reboots taking place in the middle of the night will still exist. I may have missed something of course and there may be other ways that I've not yet come across to assist with such package upgrades. It's easy to see that this area of computing evolves at a rate of knots. I, for one, will be casting my beady eye over any developments in the live kernel patching arena frequently.

Summary

The main rule of thumb is to install as few packages on your servers as possible (less is "less" in this case). I can't emphasize that point enough. Also, know what every one of your servers does. By that I mean isolate your services. For example, make sure a web server is only responsible for HTTP and keep your mail servers running on entirely separate boxes. This way, the number of sleepless nights that you'll work through will definitely be reduced. The knock-on effect is that your uptime stats will shine brightly and become a target that most other sysadmins can only aspire to.

CHAPTER 5

■ ■ ■

Get More with Wget

I frequently find myself needing to download a tarball, or a config file, to a server from a web page. Or within a script I need to know that I can query both local and remote web servers over HTTP(S) to check uptime or the presence of certain content. One of the most popular feature-filled tools is *Wget*, which, I hazard to guess, stands for "web get". Previously known as Geturl, Wget is described as "the non-interactive network downloader". It boasts several supported protocols, namely HTTP, HTTPS and FTP, and also has the ability to look past and query a site beyond HTTP proxies; a powerful feature-set indeed. But what can you use it for? In this chapter, you will explore some of its features, beginning with a few simple examples and continuing with some scenarios that you'll might find Wget the most useful.

To install Wget on Debian and Ubuntu-based systems, run the following command. There is a significant chance that it's already installed thanks to its popularity:

```
# apt-get install wget
```

To install Wget on Red Hat derivatives use the following command:

```
# yum install wget
```

Long- and Shorthand Support

The fact that Wget follows the "GNU getopt" standard means that Wget will process its command-line options in both long- and short-hand. Note the `--no-clobber` option being the same as the `-nc` option, for example. Let's see how to use Wget to download something using that option—and should that download be interrupted, you'll ask it to use the humorously named `no-clobber` option to avoid overwriting a previously downloaded file:

```
# wget –no-clobber http://www.chrisbinnie.tld
```

The same command can be run from the command line using:

```
# wget -nc http://www.chrisbinnie.tld
```

I mention this because each of the two formatting options has its place. For example, when you come to grips with the package you will likely soon be abbreviating everything and may end up inserting shorthand into a script that you've written.

However as you find your way through a package's options, it's initially much easier to write out everything in longhand. Also, if you're preparing a script that other people will be using and administrating in the future, then looking up each and every command line argument to decipher a complex command takes a reasonable amount of time. Longhand might be more suited to that situation too. Now I will try to explain each command-line option using both types of formats for clarity and to give you the choice of either.

As you might have guessed from the functionality that I've alluded to, Wget also supports "regetting" or "resuming" a download. This makes a world of difference with servers that offer such functionality. You simply pick up from the bit of the file you had already successfully downloaded, wasting no time at all to get straight back to the task at hand. And, with a 10GB file, that's usually more of a necessity than a nicety.

Logging Errors

But, what about if the marvelous Wget encounters errors during its travels? If it runs from within a script or from the command line, you can collect errors in a separate log file. A very painless solution is all that's needed and this time with the -o switch:

```
# wget --output-file logfile_for_errors http://www.chris.tld/chrisbinnie.tar.gz
```

Back to the command line. If you're not running Wget from within a script, you can drop Wget into background mode straight away after launching it. In this case, if there's no -o log file declared, then Wget will create wget-log in such cases to catch the output.

Another logging option is to append it to a log file that already exists. If you're executing a few automated scripts overnight, using Cron jobs for example, a universal Wget log file might live in the /var/log directory and get rotated by an automated log-rotation tool such as logrotate.

You can achieve this functionality with the -a option, as demonstrated here:

```
# wget –append-output=/var/log/logfile_for_errors http://www.chris.tld/chrisbinnie.tar.gz
```

While on the subject of errors and spotting what has been actioned after running Wget, you can also choose -d to enable debugging. This is simply --debug in longhand.

A minor caveat would be that some sysadmins disable this functionality by not compiling the option into Wget. If it doesn't work for you, that is likely to be the reason why.

Rather than redirect your Wget output to /dev/null all the time, you can enable -q to suppress the output. As you might have guessed, this can be enabled with the following:

```
# wget --quiet ftp://ftp.chrisbinnie.tld/largefile.tar.gz
```

There are even more options than that. Without enabling debugging, you can always use the Linux standard -v to enable the --verbose output option, which should help out most of the time. It helps diagnose simple issues at least, if things aren't quite working as you would hope.

Using the fully considered approach to which you're becoming accustomed to, the ever-trusty Wget even caters to an -nv option, which stands for --no-verbose. This allows you to disable verbose mode but without switching all noise off. As a result, you still see some simple transactional information and any useful, generated errors.

Automating Tasks

The previous features are not the only ones that make Wget so popular; it also boasts some options that, I suppose, are mainly designed for automation.

For example, -i ("input file") lets you grab not just one URL but as many as you can throw at it. You can specify a file brimming to the top with URLs using this method, as follows:

```
# wget --input-file=loads_of_links
```

You can also opt for what has been referred to as "downloading recursively" in the past. In other words, when Wget discovers a link to another page, linked to from the resource that you've pointed it at, then Wget will aim to collate a local copy of those images, files, and web pages too. Really that means anything attached to that page. The optional parameter --recursive command is as simple as -r when abbreviated:

```
# wget -r http://www.chrisbinnie.tld/inner-directory/files
```

It will pick up both HTML and XHTML. In addition, Wget thoughtfully respects the directory structures, which means, in a very handy fashion, you can essentially click through your local copy of the content as if you're surfing online.

And, a little like creating your own web content–harvesting spider, Wget will even pay attention to the standard robots.txt file commands found in the root of web sites. The robots file can instruct any automated tool, that will pay attention at least, about what is public content and allowed to be downloaded and what should be left alone. There's a whole host of other instructions, which are for another day.

As you're grabbing the content (more commonly called "scraping"), using the -i option, from within a script and saving it locally, it can also be useful to prepend a URL to the start of the resource (and any proceeding resources) with the -B option. This allows you to keep a track of which web site the resource came from. Do this by adding the top-level URL to the directory structure.

This can be achieved with:

```
--base=http://www.chrisbinnie.tld
```

A feature that I've used many times in scripts (where the content is scrutinized by grep, awk and sed once downloaded) is the -O option (not to be confused with the lowercase -o flag).

Using that option, you can drop the downloaded content to a single file and any additional downloaded content will just be appended to that file. This is rather than mimicking a downloaded web page with lots of small files in a directory.

Fulfilling Requests with Retries

One key consideration of automating any task online is accounting for the fact that there will inevitably be problems, which will cause varying degrees of pain. You should be expecting connectivity issues, outages, downtime, and general Internet malaise such as spam, bots, and malware.

You can ask that Wget dutifully try to fulfil a request by using the -t switch; or, in longhand, you can add the number of ten retries that a resource will have before Wget gives up using --tries=10. This configurable parameter really helps with poor connections or unreliable targets.

Consider a scenario where you want to pick up links and download content from HTML that's saved in a file locally. The -F or --force-html switch will allow this. Use this in the conjunction with the command switch --base to pick up relative, not absolute, links from your target.

Having touched on connectivity issues, consider this for a second. What if you have to suddenly drop your laptop into suspend mode because you've just caught sight of the time? The -c or --continue argument lets you carry on later, making the reliable Wget completely unaware that you were late for your dental appointment at 2:30.

You don't even have to add the --continue switch, as it's the default option. However, you do need it if you want to resume a download run prior to the current instance.

A super quick word of warning, however. In later versions of Wget if you ask it to kick off a "resume" on a file that already contains some content and the remote server that you connect to does not support the resume functionality, it will override the existing content in error!

To save that existing content, you should change the file name before beginning the download and then try to merge the files later.

Showing Progress

Another nice touch is a progress bar. How many times have programs just sat, looking busy even if they're not, while you wait what seems like forever?

There's no shorthand for changing the default process bar format, but fear not because adding --progress=dot will give you a counter in dots, whereas bar instead of dot will draw a perfectly plausible progress bar using ever-faithful ASCII art.

Speaking of display options, how about adding -Q? The following will let you show download details in megabytes or kilobytes (the latter in this case):

```
# wget --quote=k https://chris.binnie.tld/anotherfile.zip
```

DNS Considerations

One issue that I've encountered concerning underlying infrastructure problems in the past, and not Wget I'd like to point out, has been identified as DNS caching issues.

Back in the day, the relatively small number of domestic-market orientated ISPs were much less concerned about proxying web content to save their bandwidth. They didn't feel the need to cache popular content nearly as readily (so the content was downloaded once rather than several times, cutting down on the ISPs bandwidth usage and therefore the cost).

The same applied to Domain Name System lookups (despite DNS lookups generating a minuscule amount of traffic, there are still server-load implications). In these modern Internet times in which we live, ISPs that offer access to millions of subscribers tend to have expiry times set to much higher values (a day or two, as opposed to an hour or two, which was adequate in the past).

With Wget you can, somewhat surprisingly, disable localized caching reliance (which I should point out doesn't affect the underlying infrastructure unfortunately) to at least prevent the thoughtful Wget from causing the same caching issues every now and again. The fact that Wget is generous enough an application to provide caching in the first place is far from commonplace. Cached lookups are kept in memory only and by rerunning Wget it will mean that name servers are sent fresh queries with this option enabled.

Using Authentication

What if you can't get access to a site because it's password protected? As you might expect, Wget accounts for that common scenario too. Yet again there is more than one option for you to explore.

The most obvious way is simply entering a login and password to the command line as follows:

```
# wget --user=chris --password=binnie http://assets.chrisbinnie.tld/logo.jpg
```

But hold on for a moment. If you're aware of Bash history, never mind prying eyes, this approach is far from ideal from a security perspective.

Instead Wget lets you proffer this methodology to the command line, where you are forced to the type the password in at the prompt.

```
# wget --user=chris --ask-password http://assets.chrisbinnie.tld/logo.jpg
```

For the other main protocols, you can also throw `--ftp-user`, `--ftp-password`, `--http-user`, and `--http-password` respectively into the ring.

Denying and Crafting Cookies

If you've thought about an obvious HTTP side-effect that causes you headaches, then rest assured that Wget has it covered.

You can either deny all cookies (which collect server-side statistical information and session data) or alternatively craft them in any which way you want.

Sometimes it's necessary to carefully craft very specific cookies so that Wget can navigate a web site correctly, imitating a user for all intents and purposes. You can achieve this effect with the `--load-cookies` option. Simply add a file name as the suffix to that option and you can then effectively spoof being logged into a site by using previously generated cookie data. That means you can move around that web site with ease.

Creating Directory Structures

In and among your downloading-and-saving options are the `-nd` option, otherwise known as `--no-directories`. In addition, there's `-x`, which is its opposite (which allows you to exclude directories via comma separated list). This still allows you to create a directory structure and pull in all the followed links.

This might be useful for segmenting different data captures, even if it's only one splash page of a web site, harvested from commands that you have run from a script.

Then let's not forget adding the base URL to the beginning of the saved directories. The `-nH` or `--no-host-directories` flag lets you avoid including the base URL altogether.

Precision

And for the pedants amongst you, how about removing the mention of the protocol at the start of those saved directory names? Well, `--protocol-directories` should just save the directory as the hostname without the http, https, or ftp prepended.

I've had a problem in the past relating to how e-mail clients handled generated Character Sets from content that had been created by scripts. You can use the excellent Wget to craft headers to your heart's content. Essentially you end up creating a fake web browser header. This can be achieved as follows:

```
# wget --header='Accept-Charset: iso-2057' --header='Accept-Language: en-gb'
http://www.chrisbinnie.tld
```

Anyone who has seen their browsers complain about the maximum number of redirects being reached will see straight through this option: `--max-redirect=`. If you add a number to the end, web server redirects will generate an error once the maximum limit is exceeded. The default sits at 20.

Security

A very basic form of security is possible using the HTTP referrer field. How might it be used? A common scenario might be when a webmaster doesn't want to enable authentication to permit access to a resource, but instead wants a simple level of security added so that people can't just link directly to that end resource.

One way to do this is to enforce from which page the request came. In other words, you can only access `PageTwo.html`, for example, through a link clicked on `PageOne.html`. This loose form of security can be bypassed easily (maliciously or otherwise) by including a distinct referrer as such:

```
# wget --referrer=PageOne.html PageTwo.html
```

Posting Data

Forging onward, you can pass more complex data along the URL as if you were using a dynamic scripting language directly, such as PHP or ASP.

The `--post-data=` parameter addition lets you include a string of data such as a variable name or two with their values set, like this:

```
http://www.chrisbinnie.tld/page.php?firstname=chris&secondname=binnie.
```

There are times, however, when you'll need to pass on more data, as the Internet appears to wield lengthier URLs by the day. You can do this simply with `--post-file=` followed by a file name full of HTTP POST data. Very handy, methinks.

Ciphers

Faced with extended encryption, you can add the `--secure-protocol=name_of_protocol` parameter. You can use TLSv1 (the successor to SSL), SSLv2, or the more modern SSLv3.

You can also request "auto" instead, which enables the bundled SSL library to make an informed choice. A headache that I've had in the past has been with expired SSL certificates (from badly administrated servers) or self-signed certificates occasionally causing unusual responses. The simple fix `--no-check-certificate` is excellent for scripts and saves the day.

Initialisms

The largest files tend to live on FTP servers so it's important that Wget handles the access required to download them correctly. I'm sure you won't fall off your seat if I tell you that it surmounts this obstacle beautifully.

In addition to the `--ftp-user=chris` and `--ftp-password=binnie` parameters, the intelligent Wget will default to `-wget@`, which will satisfy anonymous FTP logins (anonymous logins are usually `login: email-address` and `password: anonymous` if you haven't come across it before).

You should be aware that you can also incorporate passwords within URLs. However, by embedding passwords inside URLs, along with the simple user and password parameters, any user on the system who runs the `ps` command to see the process table will sadly, but as if by magic, see your password. Hardly secure, I think you will agree.

You will shortly look at the predetermined named config files: `.wgetrc` or equally an alternative name is `.netrc`.

A word of warning before you get there, however. If passwords are anything but of the lowest importance, you should not leave them in plain text in either of the two config files that I just mentioned.

You can always delete them after a file download has initiated. I'm sure with some creative scripting you could unencrypt a password, drop the password into the Wget configuration file, and then dutifully remove it after the transfer has begun.

If you've come across firewalling-meets-FTP headaches in the past, I'm sure that you have heard of passive mode. You can circumvent some of these headaches by chucking the `--no-passive-ftp` option to FTP, whereas firewalls usually prefer passive mode be enabled.

If your Wget client encounters filesystem symlinks (symbolic links are a little like shortcuts on Windows for those who don't know) then sometimes it won't be presented with the actual file but it will instead look like a symlink only. As you might expect by now, however, the mighty Wget lets you decide the fate of these shortcuts with `--retr-symlinks`.

Directories that are symlinked are too painful currently for Wget to recurse through afterward, so take heed in case that causes eyestrain.

I have already mentioned the recursive `-r` option for harvesting subdirectories. A caveat is that sometimes by following links you end up with gigabyte upon gigabyte of data inadvertently. Failing that, there's a chance that you will end up with tens of thousands of tiny files (comprised of images, text files, stylesheets, and HTML) that cause administration headaches. You can explicitly specify how deep to trawl into the depths of the subdirectories with `-l` or the `--level=5`; set at five levels in this case.

Proxies

Another scenario might be as follows. You have built a proxy server that sits in between the web and your hundreds of users. You have tested it thoroughly and it's working fine but you want to fill the cache with popular web pages before hundreds of users start using the proxy server and stressing it with their sudden increase in load.

You have a whole weekend before Monday morning arrives so you decide to start copying and pasting a long list of popular URLs that will almost definitely be viewed by your users (as well as banning a few inappropriate ones). You know that you can fill a file and feed it into Wget in a variety of ways, but if you just want to visit the web sites to populate the proxy's cache, you definitely don't want to keep all of the data that you have downloaded on the machine visiting them, just within the proxy.

Wget handles this with perfect simplicity using the `--delete-after` flag. It visits the sites in a truly normal fashion (set up carefully almost like a fake web browser if required, passing the correct User Agent parameters). Once you've set that up, you simply purge all of the data that you have collected.

Fear not—this won't incur dressing-downs thanks to the accidental deletion of files on any FTP servers you visit. It is quite safe.

Mirroring

If you wanted to keep a full-fledged backup of your own web site locally, you could use Wget to scrape the content via a daily Cron job and use the `-m` or `–mirror` option.

You immediately have recursive downloading enabled by taking this approach as well as setting the directory depth to "infinite" and timestamping being enabled. For future reference, should it help, according to the man page for Wget, the mirroring feature adds the following options: `-r`, `-N`, `-l`, and `inf –no-remove-listing` in one fell swoop.

Downloading Assets

Sometimes when you're scraping a web page, the results can be disappointing. As discussed, you are effectively creating a fake browser and Wget can't possibly be expected to live up to a fully functional browser, especially with its tiny filesize footprint.

To grab all the elements that comprise a web page, you might need to enable `-p` or `--page-requisites`"= to fix this.

Within reason it makes perfect sense because the reality of today's web is one of stylesheets and highly graphical content.

One other useful feature that's worth mentioning means that (because Windows isn't usually case sensitive to file names but Unix-like operating systems are) you can choose to not pay attention to somewhat challenging, okay then irritating, file names with --ignore-case.

Persistent Config

As I mentioned, you can specify many of these parameters at runtime or from within your local user's config file. This example uses wgetrc and not .netrc.

You might always want kilobytes, for instance. And, you know that your remote file target is on an unreliable server so you always need a large number of retries before you get it right. Here's a sample .wgetrc which, in my case, would live in /home/chrisbinnie/.wgetrc.

```
Sample .wgetrc
============

quota = k # Not MegaBytes
tries = 50 # Lots of retries
reclevel = 2 # Directory levels to delve down into
use_proxy = on # Enable the proxy
https_proxy = http://proxy.chris.tld:65530/ # Set up a different proxy for each protocol
http_proxy = http://proxy.chris.tld:65531/
ftp_proxy = http://proxy.chris.tld:65532/
wait = 2 # Wait two seconds before hammering the bandwidth again
httpsonly = off # In recursive mode don't follow links which aren't HTTPS for security
secureprotocol = auto # Finely tweak your preferred encryption protocol version
```

Clearly, there are a massive amount of other options that can be included in this file. I will let you use your imagination and guile to pick and choose ones relevant to your precise requirements. Trial and error should help greatly. Once thing I love about small Linux utilities is not having to wait for a full iteration. You just press Ctrl+C if you want to interrupt a launch mid-flow.

A Note on Criminal Activity

On to a more serious note now.

I once spent a great deal of time securing a public-facing web server and for reasons that I became frustrated with I found it very difficult to avoid using an alternative to Wget called Curl.

Why did I put so much effort into avoiding such a fantastic tool being installed on my server? For the simple reason that if a small breach of my server occurred, I knew that I might be in serious trouble.

I was most concerned with the Apache web server user on the system (www-data, httpd, or even Apache being the Apache username used in the past) being exploited. I knew that Wget and Curl could be used to pull nefarious data down onto the server, which could almost certainly then be executed to take control of my server. The worst possible scenario.

You might ask why I was so sure of this threat. The simple answer is that I had witnessed precisely that type of attack in the past. If you're familiar with Apache then you'll know that as standard, without adjusting configuration settings, any hits to your web server are logged to the file /var/log/apache2/access.log. This file name changes a little, but only subtlely, depending on distribution.

While all the hits to your server end up there, any errors or informational messages are written to the /var/log/apache2/error_log file. Obviously it makes administration much easier to split the two elements into distinct files.

Having been asked to help recover one compromised server that I was helping to recover, to my absolute horror, in Apache's error log appeared a line beginning with Wget.

It was quite easy to spot because there was an extraordinary lack of timestamps at the start of each line. There were also some nonsensical characters thrown in on the lines around the handful of entries of Wget output.

It showed that this server had connected remotely to a dodgy-looking web site and the appended file name was seemingly a few random characters to disguise it. Lo and behold, this server had been compromised through a popular PHP forum application and the automated Apache user had unsuspectingly logged its activities within the error log. The sloppy attacker had not cleaned up the log files, despite gaining superuser access (so they had full permissions to tidy up and disguise their break-in route).

After some digging, I soon discovered a very nasty rootkit, which was configured to send any users' logins and passwords back to a foreign country at midnight every night. And, just in case the sysadmin for that server got wise and tried to clean the infection, there was a secondary SSH daemon running on a hidden port that didn't show up in netstat (but it did in lsof), thanks to the netstat binary being overwritten with an infection version.

Don't get me wrong—this attack was a success because of a bug in a PHP application and was far from Wget's fault. It's a word of warning for those new to security, however.

The more tools such as compilers and innocuous downloaders you leave on a server, the easier that server is to take control of even after a relatively minor breach has taken place. And, that could easily mean the difference between no extra work and three full days of rebuilding a server from scratch. If you're like me, you don't like making extra work for yourself.

Summary

A final word of warning: Don't try to scrape content illegally. As I have demonstrated, it is a very straightforward process with Wget, and Curl come to that, to take a copy of public-facing content and save it to your local drive, without breaking a sweat. However, it should go without saying that you should be aware of potential copyright headaches. At the risk of repeating a commonly spoken phrase in sysadmin circles: "With great power...".

The aim of this chapter was to stimulate some interest in the superhero that is Wget; an exceptional tool that is sometimes taken for granted. Put to good use for both diagnostic purposes and a multitudinous variety of scripts, Wget is a fantastic weapon that should be included in any sysadmin's arsenal. With some creative thinking, I trust that you will enjoy experimenting with Wget as much as I have.

CHAPTER 6

■ ■ ■

SECURING SSH with PAM

There's little argument that SSH (and in particular the OpenSSH implementation) is the remote access method of choice for Unix-type machines connected to the Internet and to local networks. At times, however, it's just not convenient to have your SSH key readily available and present on the device that you're logging in from. If you've ever had to type an SSH key in manually, in order to copy it from one device to another, you know it's a little like trying to push water up a hill. It's not recommended.

This is where two-step (or two-factor) authentication comes in. Coupled with the already excellent security that SSH provides and a pluggable module compatible with most Linux flavors, courtesy of search giant Google, the superiorly secure Google Authenticator can mean that even if you're not using SSH keys, your logins are much safer. I'm referring to mitigating brute-force attacks on your passwords and the like.

In this chapter, you learn how to harden your SSH server configuration by adding TCP wrappers (so that only IP addresses or domain names that you trust can log in). You'll finish off by enabling the Google authenticator library to add two-step (or two-factor) authentication. Google Authenticator supports a number of devices including iPhone, iPod Touch, iPad, and BlackBerry. As Google's own smartphone brand is Android, and other versions are ports of the Android version, this chapter focuses on that device. Other than the package installation on your smartphone, however, the rest of the information should apply. To install the package for a device other than Android, simply select your device from this web page and follow the instructions: https://support.google.com/accounts/answer/1066447?hl=en.

A Note About Standards

If you're new to the technicalities of how the standards on the Internet work then a quick mention of RFCs is probably needed. RFCs are "Request For Comments," which the Internet Engineering Task Force (IETF) publishes along with the Internet Society (ISoc). Think of each RFC as a specification of each standard put together by those who know best for discussion or adoption by the Internet communities to whom they relate. I mention RFCs because the Google Authenticator utility available on Linux is based on Initiative for Open Authentication (OATH) standards (http://www.openauthentication.org), not to be confused with the popular OAuth (http://oauth.net). Furthermore, don't think of the Google Authenticator Android App as being the same thing as the Linux project of the same name. They are quite separate entities (more on the Android incarnation is here: https://github.com/google/google-authenticator-android).

Google Authenticator supports two RFCs: The HMAC-Based One-Time Password (HOTP) algorithm, which is specified in RFC 4226 (https://tools.ietf.org/html/rfc4226) and the Time-Based One-Time Password (TOTP) algorithm, which is specified in RFC 6238 (https://tools.ietf.org/html/rfc6238). Both documents are worth a quick skim through. It's a good learning experience even if you're just picking up new terminology.

That's enough theory, let's focus on getting your SSH server secured more robustly by running Google Authenticator (https://github.com/google/google-authenticator).

Configuring Your SSH Server

A quick summary of the key changes that you should be making to your /etc/ssh/sshd_config file. You can, as ever, go further than just applying these changes, but they are a good starting point in most cases. What follows are my personal preferences and what I would consider a minimum.

You have to modify a few lines in your config file. Begin by identifying the following lines in your config file and then alter them to reflect the following settings or add them if they're not present.

- Change your SSH server port so that automated attacks don't fill your logs with quite as much noise like this:

```
Port 2222
```

- Avoid the weaker version 1 protocol by only allowing clients running the second version to connect with this line:

```
Protocol 2
```

- Ensure that only less-privileged users can connect initially over SSH like this:

```
PermitRootLogin No
```

- Ensure that only usernames that you explicitly allow are allowed to log in. I leave this setting at the top of the config file to immediately point out that it's enabled when troubleshooting a problem. That way, I see it as soon as I open the file.

```
AllowUsers chrisbinnie sysadmin
```

  - I haven't tried the following more advanced syntax, but (carefully, without closing your existing SSH session) you might want to test these examples too. Here the user neymar can only connect from the IP address 10.10.10.10; user lionel can connect from any machine; and the user luis must connect from machines with a hostname under the chrisbinnie.tld domain name, such as barca.chrisbinnie.tld:

```
AllowUsers neymar@10.10.10.10 lionel luis@*.chrisbinnie.tld
```

  - Lots of users might be more manageable with a group (I won't include it in this config however), which could be achieved like this:

```
AllowGroup sysops
```

- Next, verify that the following setting is disabled. When establishing a remote connection, you tend to trust the client that you're connecting from more than the server that you're connecting to and therefore don't accept X11 communications unless they're specifically needed.

```
X11Forwarding no
```

- It's unlikely to be disabled, but check this config setting just in case:

  UsePAM yes

- Now quickly check that this option is also enabled:

  ChallengeResponseAuthentication yes

- And finally, although not strictly security related and more of a throwback, don't wait for hideously long DNS timeouts during a connection by using this setting:

  UseDNS no

Now it's time to face your daemons and restart your SSH service, using the following command (on newer systems that run systemd):

```
# systemctl restart sshd.service
```

At this stage it's not a bad idea to try to log in from different IP addresses and as different users so that you have confidence in your newly configured security before potentially making it more complex with two-step authentication. If you're seriously unsure of any of the above (or can't get it working), then you may want to move over to a development machine. Or at the very least, go to a machine that you can physically log in to via a terminal or one that has a virtual console available, such as a virtual machine or cloud instance. In other words, you might need an out-of-band login prompt of some description that doesn't rely on your SSH server.

Wrapping Your Connections

Next, you'll wrap up your SSH connections by making sure that only specific domain names or IP addresses (or ranges of IP addresses) can connect.

This is very simple but a word of caution is in order. Don't close your existing SSH connection until you've tested that your new config has worked. You can do this by spawning a new SSH session. You might be locked out otherwise; believe me when I say that it's easy to do, even for old-timers. I prefer to use TCP wrappers for tasks such as these because the likelihood of typing errors is greatly reduced. At the end of this section you can see an IPtables example if you prefer to go that route. Open the file /etc/hosts.allow and add something along these lines:

```
sshd: .chrisbinnie.tld
sshd: 123.123.123.0/24
```

I've separated the lines for the purposes of demonstrating the differences in the syntax. On the top line, notice the important preceding dot before the domain name chrisbinnie.tld. Here any machine with a hostname that falls under that domain name will be allowed to connect, similar to the config used directly as an example in the more advanced SSH config. Similarly, on the second line, any of the 254 IP addresses within the 123.123.123.0 range will also be given access. I tend to prefer raw IP addresses in this file as a rule because DNS entries can be spoofed. IP addresses are much trickier.

The excellent TCP wrappers hosts.allow file is too clever for words and you can also include slightly odd-looking settings such as this:

```
sshd: 10.10.
```

Here the many IP addresses that begin with `10.10.` are allowed access. This leaves access relatively open, so be sure to use a setting like this with caution.

Don't just think that TCP wrappers apply to your SSH server only, of course; look at the following example, which includes a netmask for all services that support TCP wrappers (further details can be found at `http://www.admin-magazine.com/Articles/Secure-Your-Server-with-TCP-Wrappers`):

```
ALL: 10.10.0.0/255.255.254.0
```

In order to make these changes live, you need to edit the file `/etc/hosts.deny`. Remember not to close your existing SSH session until you're happy that you can log in successfully again! Add this line to the deny file:

```
sshd: ALL
```

Equally you might of course opt to secure your SSH server using `IPtables` too. I will leave you to look up which option suits your needs but this shown below works for me.

```
# iptables -A INPUT -i eth0 -p tcp -s 123.123.123.0/24 --dport 2222 -m state --state
NEW,ESTABLISHED -j ACCEPT
# iptables -A OUTPUT -o eth0 -p tcp --sport 2222 -m state --state ESTABLISHED -j ACCEPT
```

Getting Started with Two-Step Authentication

Now that you can ensure that only select users are allowed to log in over SSH, and from very specific IP addresses or machines, it's time to get your hands dirty with two-step authentication. Using the excellent pluggable authentication modules provided by PAM, Google Authenticator supports the following features, according to its GitHub page (`https://github.com/google/google-authenticator/wiki`):

- Per-user secret and status file stored in the user's home directory

- Support for 30-second TOTP codes

- Support for emergency scratch codes

- Protection against replay attacks

- Key provisioning via display of a QRCode

- Manual key entry of RFC 3548 (`http://tools.ietf.org/html/rfc3548`) base32 key strings

I love the mention of "scratch codes." These can be used during a break-glass-in-an-emergency style scenario so that you're never locked out completely (in theory). Let's have a look at some of the terminology and one feature in particular before getting lost in setting it up.

I mentioned the TOTP (time-orientated) codes earlier. Consider what would happen if a code which you had generated was wrong because of a difference in client and server time settings. The server simply wouldn't trust the code and all hell would break loose as you were locked out.

There's some leeway given for time skew, but there's also a clever option for helping to mitigate expected issues. You might not have your client device connected to an NTP (Network Time Protocol) server, for example, or you could be connecting remotely from a location where network latency plays a part in the opening handshake. Rather than lower the security integrity of the authentication mechanism, the pluggable module listens intently as the user fails repeatedly to authenticate successfully. The user is obviously going to be frustrated entering what they think are valid codes. After three attempts, when the option is enabled, the PAM module takes time for time skew and measures the device's misjudged attempts in order to compensate. It then lets the user connect if appropriate. Clever, huh?

Near the end of the smartphone package installation process, you will be asked questions relating to the time settings. Thankfully the queries are relatively detailed so I will leave you to choose the best options for your circumstances.

Installing the Required Packages

If you want to install the required packages via a package manager, then try this on Debian derivatives (I'm on "Jessie"):

```
# apt-get install libpam-google-authenticator
```

Figure 6-1 shows the installation process in a little more detail.

```
Reading package lists... Done
Building dependency tree
Reading state information... Done
The following NEW packages will be installed:
  libpam-google-authenticator libqrencode3
0 upgraded, 2 newly installed, 0 to remove and 0 not upgraded.
Need to get 65.8 kB of archives.
After this operation, 216 kB of additional disk space will be used.
Get:1 http://http.debian.net/debian/ jessie/main libqrencode3 amd64 3.4.3-1 [33.8 kB]
Get:2 http://http.debian.net/debian/ jessie/main libpam-google-authenticator amd64 20130529-2 [32.1 kB]
Fetched 65.8 kB in 0s (260 kB/s)
Selecting previously unselected package libqrencode3:amd64.
(Reading database ... 36818 files and directories currently installed.)
Preparing to unpack .../libqrencode3_3.4.3-1_amd64.deb ...
Unpacking libqrencode3:amd64 (3.4.3-1) ...
Selecting previously unselected package libpam-google-authenticator.
Preparing to unpack .../libpam-google-authenticator_20130529-2_amd64.deb ...
Unpacking libpam-google-authenticator (20130529-2) ...
Processing triggers for man-db (2.7.0.2-5) ...
Setting up libqrencode3:amd64 (3.4.3-1) ...
Setting up libpam-google-authenticator (20130529-2) ...
Processing triggers for libc-bin (2.19-18+deb8u1) ...
Scanning processes...
Scanning candidates...
Scanning kernel images...
Running kernel seems to be up-to-date.
Restarting services using systemd...
```

Figure 6-1. *Detailed installation information of the PAM module*

If you're so inclined, you can also download the source from GitHub at https://github.com/google/google-authenticator/ and then change (cd) to the directory where you've saved and unpacked the download. Then use these commands:

```
# ./bootstrap.sh
# ./configure
# make; make install
```

It's probably safer to be the "root" user (at least for the make install command) to run these commands. Next, you need to add the following line to the bottom of the PAM config file. On Debian and Red Hat, that file can most likely be found at /etc/pam.d/sshd.

```
auth required pam_google_authenticator.so
```

You probably want to add a comment above that line in keeping with the neatness of the file in general. As a result, it looks more like this:

```
# Google Authenticator for PAM - add a comment to the following line to disable it and then
restart sshd
auth required pam_google_authenticator.so
```

Next, restart SSH. On newer versions of Linux running systemd such as Debian "Jessie," you can use the following:

```
# systemctl restart sshd.service
```

After that you're all set to try your new security implementation. Another reminder that you shouldn't log out of any SSH sessions you have in use!

Installing Google Authenticator On Android

Before jumping ahead, you need to search the Google Play App Store for "google authenticator" or simply "authenticator" and then install the relevant app on your Android phone (the required instructions for installing Google Authenticator on other devices is here: https://support.google.com/accounts/answer/1066447?hl=en).

Back to your SSH server. If your system supports the libqrencode library (it's called libqrencode3 in Debian Jessie's repositories and can be checked with apt-get install libqrencode3), then you should be shown a QRCode on your console. Your Android Phone app is primed to scan a QRCode to save you typing in a code manually if you desire (you may need another small barcode-reading app installed, but the operating system should tell you if this is so).

If your system doesn't support QRCodes, it's just a case of typing an alphanumeric code into your smartphone's app, which is a little tedious but thankfully nothing too taxing.

Once the code is entered you should see a single code changing every few seconds (the timer is the blue circle on the right), as shown in Figure 6-2. (In case you're wondering, I tend to obfuscate as many things relating to security as I can, hence the odd names under the codes in Figure 6-2 and not "My Bank Account's secret code.")

Figure 6-2. *On this display, two servers are updating their codes every few seconds*

Back to your SSH server. Logged in as an allowed SSH user (one of those select usernames that can log in under "AllowUsers" in your SSH config), you now run the following command:

```
# google-authenticator
```

As shown in Figure 6-3, you don't need X Windows or any fancy desktop manager software to display your QRCode at installation time.

Figure 6-3. *What you see having run the command* google-authenticator *as the user that you want to log in over SSH with*

After the QRCode, you will also be presented with the secret key and emergency scratch codes. The secret key comprises of the characters hidden in the QRCode, so simply type that into your Android device if you're not scanning the QRCode.

Note also that you have just disabled SSH access for the "root" user, so there should never be any good reason to run the google-authenticator command as the superuser. Instead make sure that you become another user (run a command such as su - chrisbinnie) so that you don't log out of your working SSH session until you're happy with testing and then run the command. The result is that you'll have a miniscule file written to your home directory containing your user's token.

Testing SSH Access

Remember: You still want to keep any existing SSH sessions open while you test your access so that you're not locked out. By connecting over SSH, you should now see something like the following prompts:

```
# cb@chrisbox:~$ ssh -p 2222 -l chrisbinnie prodserver1.chrisbinnie.tld
Password:
Verification code:
```

The `Verification code:` prompt is a new addition to your normal login process over SSH. If all is going well, you should only be able to get access with your password and a time-limited code. If that's the case, then try getting the code wrong so that you're used to the errors that are generated.

Summary

You now have solid SSH server security in place to help keep the wolves at bay. You've changed the port number most likely to be hit by automated attacks and additionally locked down three key aspects of anyone logging in over SSH. You've limited the usernames that can be used to enter a password at the SSH login prompt. And, that's of course based on the premise that the users has been shown the prompt in the first place because they have connected via one of the few IP addresses (or hostnames) that are permitted to open up a session on the SSH port. Finally, if those two criteria are met then a uniquely generated, time limited, access code is required to gain any access to the system. All in, that's a pretty robust front door with chunky locks and bolts to keep it firmly closed to anyone who comes knocking without credentials.

The only other addition that immediately springs to mind to further bolster the network-facing aspect of an SSH server (without using SSH keys) is the addition of a technique called *port knocking* (http://www.admin-magazine.com/Archive/2014/23/Port-Knocking). You might be surprised to learn that you can make your SSH port entirely invisible to port scans and the Internet at large. The only way to remove its invisibility cloak is to knock on other TCP or UDP ports, in a pre-configured sequence, and then as if by magic, port 2222 will appear like an apparition and allow your clients to connect.

With your newly found knowledge, I hope that you can rest assured that your SSH server is fully locked down and remote access over SSH to your boxes should only be possible by you or those who you permit. One thing to note, however, is to keep an eye on your emergency scratch codes, just in case. Not all servers can be logged into from a physical console these days.

CHAPTER 7

■ ■ ■

Your Disks, Your Way

After adding a new drive to a server or even a workstation, if you're like me there's always a few minutes of familiar trepidation as you remind yourself of how the fdisk utility works. If you mess up, you can render your server's main drive unusable or put your desktop's backup drive into an irreparable state. There are ways of recovering deleted partitions, but frankly I've got other things to be getting on with. Even when your heart rate is back to normal, having mastered the required partitioning task, you're not over the finish line yet because you still have to figure out the best filesystem for the job at hand.

Most Linux distributions periodically announce that they've moved from a previously favored (default) filesystem to a newer one every few version releases. Clearly this is how software, services, and ultimately systems evolve and, if there have been sufficient levels of testing, these advancements should be warmly welcomed. This chapter covers the requisite steps after running your favorite partition manipulation tool, for example fdisk as I mentioned earlier, to help set up and tune your drives. A little consideration is required because before you can use your shiny new drives you need to think about formatting them correctly and then how you might expect to fill them up with data later on.

Creating a Filesystem

I suspect that Windows users (not admins I hasten to add) tend to just click "Quick Format" when a new USB drive is attached and don't really even think about any potential consequences having chosen FAT or NTFS. The "Quick Format" function simply creates a new file table and doesn't actually delete any of the data on the drive, which takes much longer.

Clicking here and pointing there on Windows is all well and good, but how do you get a drive ready on Unix-type operating systems, having sized up a preferred partition sizes with the fdisk utility?

The first tool I'll discuss is an old friend of Unix, heralding from the mkfs days: mke2fs. Part of the e2fsprogs package, this clever utility means that you can format any drive using the latest members of the "extended filesystems" family. ext2 or the "second extended filesystem" is the grandfather of the widely supported mke2fs filesystems. It is a well-trusted, fast filesystem that I remember always using for my root partitions for boot speed when ext3 was ruling the roost. At the time of writing, ext4 is the reigning king.

The main difference between the two older versions is that ext3 is a journaling filesystem, which means after a crash or power failure the chances of recovering data on disks are significantly greater. There should also be less filesystem checks such as those associated with running fsck fairly frequently on ext2 filesystems

To see which filesystems are currently in use, type the following command:

```
# mount
```

Listing 7-1 is an abbreviated output, showing you which filesystems are in use on my machine. In this example, the boot drive /dev/sda1 is using ext4.

Listing 7-1. An Abbreviated Listing of the Types of Filesystems My Machine Uses

```
proc on /proc type proc (rw)
sysfs on /sys type sysfs (rw)
devpts on /dev/pts type devpts (rw,gid=5,mode=620)
tmpfs on /dev/shm type tmpfs (rw,noexec,nosuid,nodev,rootcontext="system_u:object_r:tmpfs_t:s0")
/dev/sda1 on /boot type ext4 (rw,noexec,nosuid,nodev)
```

The mke2fs Options.

The options available to the mke2fs utility are plentiful but it's not rocket science to get mke2fs working as efficiently.

The two key parameters are that of the partition name followed by blocks-count and the latter can be ignored if you want the mke2fs utility to automatically work out the filesystem size using its sophistication. Just specify the partition name as follows and this will dutifully format the partition /dev/sdb2. Use it carefully!

```
# mke2fs /dev/sdb2
```

If you look at the contents of the file /etc/mke2fs.conf (see Listing 7-2), you can see how the Linux distribution prefers to configure the activities of the mke2fs utility by default. You can see, for example, that the feature selected for ext3 filesystems is has_journal, whereas the new kid on the block (pun intended, sigh) has many features included by default.

Listing 7-2. The Config Shown Contains the Innards of the /etc/mke2fs.conf File

```
[defaults]
        base_features = sparse_super,filetype,resize_inode,dir_index,ext_attr
        blocksize = 4096
        inode_size = 256
        inode_ratio = 16384

[fs_types]
        ext3 = {
                features = has_journal
        }
        ext4 = {
                features = has_journal,extent,huge_file,flex_bg,uninit_bg,dir_nlink,
                extra_isize
                inode_size = 256
        }
        ext4dev = {
                features = has_journal,extent,huge_file,flex_bg,uninit_bg,dir_nlink,
                extra_isize
                inode_size = 256
                options = test_fs=1
        }
```

```
small = {
        blocksize = 1024
        inode_size = 128
        inode_ratio = 4096
}
floppy = {
        blocksize = 1024
        inode_size = 128
        inode_ratio = 8192
}
news = {
        inode_ratio = 4096
}
largefile = {
        inode_ratio = 1048576
        blocksize = -1
}
largefile4 = {
        inode_ratio = 4194304
        blocksize = -1
}
hurd = {
      blocksize = 4096
      inode_size = 128
}
```

There's always much ado about "inode ratios," which I will look at in more detail next.

Handling Index Node Problems

Let us consider a very worrying scenario the first time that you encounter it. You might come across inode problems when your operating system suddenly complains about running out of space, even though there's loads of capacity left.

How could a disk complain it's out of space when there's 50GB left? On top of surprising and unwanted error messages, usually first thing on a Monday morning, there's another pretty nasty gotcha relating to inodes.

The "index node" or "inode" is the destination that a file on your filesystem ultimately links to. The same applies for directories. Don't get confused here with file descriptors, which essentially refer to kernel pointers for open files (those that are in use).

The key issue is that, a little like disk space itself, inodes are also a finite commodity (thanks to performance issues) and therefore limited by design.

It's pretty straightforward. When you create a new file it is given a name and an inode number. That number is unique on the filesystem and directories themselves are responsible for storing details about which file relates to which inode number. On Unix-type systems a filename is just a pointer to an inode number, which is pulled from a reference table. Any software or system function that needs to use a file uses this table to find out its unique number.

It might be nice to have loads of extra inodes available but sadly the rule of thumb is that a large number of inodes increases the space that the inode table will consume, reducing how much disk space is left for usage and potentially impacting overall disk IO performance as the table is referenced so much.

It's a simple case of quid pro quo. With all types of systems there are overheads introduced when you lean further in one direction over another. When you add security measures to accessing your server, your login time is the overhead, for example, and when you add more software to a system to provide more features, there are more package upgrades to keep an eye on. The same applies here.

Listing 7-3 provides an example of how inodes look in relation to your filesystem. It shows the abbreviated output of the df -i command showing how these filesystems were set up to deal with inodes. As opposed to the usual df command, you can see inode capacities on used and available disk space.

Listing 7-3. The Output of the "df -i" Command

Filesystem	Inodes	IUsed	IFree	IUse%	Mounted on
tmpfs	490578	1	490577	1%	dev/shm
/dev/sdb2	128016	50	127966	1%	/boot

For the total inode in use on a filesystem, you can also use the excellent tune2fs tool (run as the "root" user), as shown in the following command (more on this powerful utility later in this chapter).

```
# tune2fs -l /dev/sdb2 | grep -i "inode count"
```

Dealing with Problematic Files

Should you ever get caught when trying to delete a file with a bizarre file name (you know the type with seemingly endless, obscure characters in their names?) that has been created by a misbehaving piece of software, you can use its inode to delete it. You can find out an "index number" of a file by using this command with the -i switch:

```
# ls -il

518 -rw-rw-r--. 1 chrisbinnie chrisbinnie 361 Feb 17 13:13 chris.pp
```

The arbitrary file that I've chosen to look at here belongs to the venerable Puppet and you can see that this manifest file has the inode 518. You can also use the helpful stat command like this:

```
# stat chris.pp
```

Listing 7-4 shows what the stat command reveals about the file chris.pp.

Listing 7-4. The "stat" command confirms the inode number for the Puppet Manifest "chris.pp" Is indeed 518

```
Size: 361       Blocks: 8      IO Block: 4096    regular file
Device: ae12h/44257e    Inode: 518         Links: 1
Access: (0664/-rw-rw-r--)  Uid: (172829418/ chrisbinnie)   Gid: (172829201/ chrisbinnie)
Access: 2015-03-03 13:00:57.974669752 +0100
Modify: 2015-03-03 13:13:06.590592150 +0100
Change: 2015-03-03 13:13:06.590592150 +0100
```

If you want to delete that file by referencing its inode, you can use the find command as follows (be sure to test it on a development machine first):

```
# find . -inum 518 -exec rm -i {} \;
```

Assuming that all makes sense, then let's get back to the matter in hand. Coming into work on a Monday morning and suddenly receiving all sorts of flak because a production server has run out of disk space and fallen over might be even less pleasant than you might at first think (if its inode related).

The key issue here is that in order to change the number of inodes on a partition, you need to format the drive if it's a member of the ext family of filesystems! All you can do to bring your precious production server back online (quickly) is to either delete a whack of files (to free up some inodes) or move lots of files to a different partition and create a symlink to those files from your problem partition.

There's something else that you might consider and that's looking at what is actually using all those valuable inodes. The culprits are likely to be either lots of tiny files or long file names (or both).

Rest assured there is some remedial action that you can take. Here are a couple of commands that might save the day, assuming that you know which offending directories are full of little files in great number. This command will show you how many files are in a directory and pipe it into less:

```
# for culprits in /home/chrisbinnie/*; do echo $culprits; find $culprits | wc -l; done | less
```

Among the chaff you might see something wheaty, like this buried in the output:

```
/home/chrisbinnie/thumbnails
31,313
```

In order to delete those pesky thumbnail files, you could carefully use the following command and then run a df -i once more:

```
# rm -rf /home/chrisbinnie/thumbnails
```

Incidentally, if you spot the same inode number more than once, then fear not, it is still unique but in this case has been created by a hard link. Rather than duplicating content on a filesystem, different file names simply point at the same inode for efficiency.

Shorter File Names Are Better

Remember that I also mentioned there's a problem with lengthy file names too? This headache is seemingly less well-known relative to the "many small files" issue. Here's how it works.

Files that have between 1 and 16 characters in their name use one inode. The next level up is from 17 to 32, which counts as two inodes. From 33 to 48 characters, each file name tallies up a massive three inodes, etc.

This simple but slightly alarming equation means that the longer your file names, the fewer files you can have.

Formatting A Partition

Back to your freshly provisioned disk for a moment now.

When you're ready to format your new partition with a shiny new filesystem, you might consider adding a "usage-type" option to the mke2fs command. Have a quick peek at Listing 7-2 and consider the fs_types on show.

A reminder that a bog-standard ext4 formatting command would look like this (used carefully, with the correct partition name of course):

```
# mkfs.ext4 /dev/sdb2
```

If you add one of the fs_types from Listing 7-2 to that command as a "usage-type" then you can put the following syntax to good use:

```
# mkfs.ext4 -T <usage-type> /dev/sdb2
```

The beefiest "usage-type" in terms of a high number of inodes (referred to as a ratio) appears to be called "news". I won't profess to understand all the ins and outs but by way of a yardstick, on a one terabyte drive (1 TB) you might expect around 244 million inodes.

An alternative to using a no-going-back filesystem is choosing a next-generation filesystem such as btrfs. These newer filesystems introduce features such as being able to make inode count changes on the fly.

Sadly without such functionality provided by the likes of btrfs, there are a few (debatable) concerns if you're faced with increasing the number of inodes using an estimated level on ext filesystems. Simply put, if you go ahead and blindly bump up the number of inodes without thinking about the tradeoffs, these headaches might rear their head, now or in the future:

- You might introduce an exponential increase in fsck runtimes (at boot time and when used to recover from corruption issues), which might jump from 30 seconds all the way up to a number of days; far from ideal for production server uptime.

- It is possible to tune ext4 "block sizes" to improve performance, but that in turn increases the number of required inodes.

- Directory listing for users may suffer from performance degradation, as would be the case with applications that access the filesystem such as software repositories.

- More RAM might be used, as the inode table is larger and as a result more files might be kept open.

As I'm sure you will agree, these issues provide a supporting argument to encourage the use of logical volumes. With logical volumes you can almost instantaneously apply disk capacity from a pool of predefined space to a partition struggling with inode or disk capacity.

With such an approach, you could allocate 10GB of new space to a busy partition periodically. It's prudent to also inform your developers, or equally configure your application in such a way, to use shorter file names where it is sensible and opt for slightly larger consolidated files rather than thousands of little files.

Formatting Option

Covering all formatting options is beyond the scope of this book. Here, I will just discuss a small sample to get you started and I encourage you to explore these options further.

If you use the -j switch, then journaling is enabled as if using mkfs.ext3; in other words, the following two commands yield the same result:

```
# mkfs.ext3 /dev/sdb2
```

```
# mk2fs -j /dev/sdb2
```

Ditto for ext2 minus the -j option, as it doesn't support journaling.

The -m option stands for "reserved-blocks-percentage" and this setting offers a feature specifically for the superuser or "root" user. Using this feature, you can reserve blocks on a drive should it fill up so that critical services can keep running. As standard, five percent of a formatted drive is given as an allocation.

Picture a scenario when your latest Elasticsearch or Kibana installation is putting the squeeze on your available disk space and /var/log is also on the same partition. If your syslog daemon is writing to the same drive and can't continue writing logs then bad things can happen.

However, because syslog is running with root privileges, it is allowed to function correctly, at least until manual intervention is possible, by populating the reserved disk space. Clever, huh?

It is recommended that for both the "root" and "home" partitions, the default five percent is the very minimum reserved. If only straightforward data will be written to a partition, then that can be reduced to the minimum of one percent with some comfort.

Personally I would increase the /var or /var/log partitions to higher than that. Bear in mind not to go too crazy, after all on a 500GB drive the default five percent is already eating up a non-trivial 25GB of space.

In the years to come, we're likely to see more advanced filesystems being used more and more. Newer emerging filesystems include btrfs. Its name is a derivative of "B-tree filesystem" but it's often pronounced as "better FS". It introduces a number of features, thus improving scalability and stability. You can snapshot a partition and compress data too. Another high-performance alternative is called XFS (a 64-bit journaling filesystem created by Silicon Graphics Inc).

If you were to create a new partition and wanted to format them using btrfs or XFS, for example, you'd use the mkfs command as follows:

```
# mkfs.btrfs /dev/sda1
```

```
# mkfs.xfs /dev/sdb2
```

Using tune2fs

I briefly mentioned the excellent tune2fs utility earlier. When you run the same command as earlier but without including the grep command, you get the output shown in Listing 7-5.

```
# tune2fs -l /dev/sda1
```

Listing 7-5. The Output of the "tune2fs -l /dev/sda1" Command

```
Filesystem volume name:    <none>
Last mounted on:           /boot
Filesystem UUID:           0612ce28-126a-32a1-db18-c2b5a3c988
Filesystem magic number:   0xEF53
Filesystem revision #:      1 (dynamic)
Filesystem features:       has_journal ext_attr resize_inode dir_index filetype needs_
recovery extent flex_bg sparse_super huge_file uninit_bg dir_nlink extra_isize
Filesystem flags:          signed_directory_hash
Default mount options:     user_xattr acl
Filesystem state:          clean
Errors behavior:           Continue
Filesystem OS type:        Linux
Inode count:               128016
Block count:               512000
Reserved block count:      25600
Free blocks:               420841
Free inodes:               127966
First block:               1
Block size:                1024
Fragment size:             1024
Reserved GDT blocks:       256
Blocks per group:          8192
Fragments per group:       8192
```

```
Inodes per group:          2032
Inode blocks per group:    254
Flex block group size:     16
Filesystem created:        Mon Nov 11 11:11:11 2011
Last mount time:           Thu Jan 3 13:31:31 2013
Last write time:           Thu Nov 11 11:11:11 2011
Mount count:               5
Maximum mount count:       -1
Last checked:              Mon Mar 1 13:31:13 2013
Check interval:            0 (<none>)
Lifetime writes:           67 MB
Reserved blocks uid:       0 (user root)
Reserved blocks gid:       0 (group root)
First inode:               15
Inode size:                108
Journal inode:             8
Default directory hash:    half_md4
Directory Hash Seed:       abf5a1b2-db11-c2b5a3c988-db18-c2b5a3c988
Journal backup:            inode blocks
```

The tune2fs utility offers the ability to alter any of the tunable settings on the now familiar ext2, ext3, and ext4 filesystems. As is apparent in Listing 7-5, tune2fs is capable of outputting lots of useful information, including inodes and the drive's UUID among a plethora of useful config settings.

The highly useful disk space reservation for extra-curricular activities on this particular partition is shown as follows in Listing 7-5:

```
Reserved block count: 25600
```

Other salient entries from that very lengthy output are the UID and GID lines:

```
Reserved blocks uid:       0 (user root)
Reserved blocks gid:       0 (group root)
```

The user and group settings above show who is allowed to use the reservation and can be altered to reflect a different user or group especially suited to its use if need be.

If you wanted to adjust that setting (even though you've populated your drive with data), you can use this command:

```
# tune2fs -m 10 /dev/sda1
```

Here we have adjusted the standard 5 percent to 10 percent of reserved space. This is an extremely helpful setting in some circumstances.

Using fsck

The filesystem consistency check utility known as fsck tends to be more suited to non-journaling filesystems, such as ext2, but it can save the day for the other family members too. fsck is the friend you want on your side when your server won't boot. If your disk is borked then try this in the first instance:

```
# fsck /dev/sdb2
```

If the drive has balked so badly that fsck can't even tell what type of filesystem is present, you might need to give it a hand, as so:

```
# fsck -t ext3 /dev/sdb2
```

Reminder: You will need to "umount /dev/sdb2" prior to using fsck.

If you've ever had any serious headaches with a drive and used fsck, you're likely to have been scrambling for the -y option. And, if you couldn't find it, you wished that it existed. I have to admit I have a mental block with this option and always resort to having to look it up.

You may indeed ask why the lifesaver that is fsck asks so many questions when it is running. It's because fsck is extremely concerned about losing your valuable data as it tries to recover access to your filesystem. It is after all considered a tool of last resort when all else is likely to have failed to automatically recover your filesystem to a useful state.

The excellent utility is quite capable of asking a hundred questions about moving this fragment of data here or saving this fragment from there during a single execution. The magical -y switch means that it will still try its absolute hardest to please the sysadmin and effectively answer "yes" to every question. Never forget this option! Really.

The fsck command can be used as simply as this and your computer can be left to run fsck on its own, thereafter without intervention:

```
# fsck -y /dev/sdb2
```

The utility will try to pick up the pieces of partially deleted files (which you would have otherwise lost entirely). After fsck has run, you should look in the directory /home/lost+found for any nearly recovered data. You never know what you might find.

There's a useful --noop or --dry-run equivalent, but in the case of fsck this is written as -N, as follows:

```
# fsck -N /dev/sdb2
```

Here very sensibly you'll only see what would have been done, as a dry run. You can put this option to good use before risking data loss and treat it as preflight check.

Summary

Having covered a few different tools, it is my hope that you are now armed with enough information to tune your disks to your preference. There are many other options to explore with all the packages covered here.

Whether it's making sure that your syslog server is capable of surviving a user going overboard with disk usage, or you need to quickly delete lots of small files, your new knowledge might just save the day at some point in the future. There are always data and backup issues that arise when you least expect it and usually when you are at your busiest.

Finally, the -y switch for fsck is a godsend when you need to get a production system back online quickly. I'm no longer taken by surprise at how many years old some Unix-like boxes are; you know the ones that are in production and haven't had a reboot for two years. I look forward to running fsck -y via a physical console on an unhappy ext2 filesystem, in order to help a server boot up again, in another few years time. I'll have to remember to warn the customer about inode limitations too.

CHAPTER 8

■ ■ ■

No sFTP Doesn't Mean No Encryption

Accessing Unix-like servers remotely is almost universally done these days by SSH (Secure Shell). SSH is so popular that the rare times that it isn't used (and something like a Telnet client is used instead) must show up on graphs as the tiniest of the smallest fractions of a percent. Personally, I rarely use SCP (Secure Copy); instead I use sFTP (Secure File Transfer Protocol) for most of my manual file transfers. The clever sFTP functionality runs as a subsystem of SSH, which adds encryption to the old-school file transfer protocol (FTP) to keep login details and transactional information safer during transit.

Sometimes, however, you find yourself feeling frustrated because you don't have SSH or sFTP available to you at one end of a connection. During those times, you need a simple command-line tool that lets you use FTP from a Unix-type command line over the Internet, but securely. In this chapter, you'll look at a natty little piece of software called lftp, which allows you to encrypt file transfers without using SSH. I'll examine a few different scenarios, so that you're suitably armed, in the event that one day you discover that SSH is unavailable to you because you're working from inside a closed environment or you have an insecure SSH version that you can't upgrade for some reason.

Using lftp

First, you'll look at connecting to a server that supports an encrypted version of FTP that isn't actually sFTP, in the SSH sense of the definition, but rather FTPS (which reportedly covers FTP-ES, FTP-SSL, and FTP Secure). FTP-ES explicitly (note the "E" for explicit) demands that encryption is used, whereas FTPS implies that encryption should be used.

One of the secure FTP options that I frequently turn to is called lftp and, according to its manual, it "can handle several file access methods—ftp, ftps, http, https, hftp, fish, sftp, and file (https and ftps are only available when lftp is compiled with GNU TLS or OpenSSL library)." This is an impressive range of protocols for any small utility, indeed. The only caveat that springs to mind is firewalling—unlike ftp, FTPS doesn't use the network port 21, but instead it uses port 990 by default.

Installation

On Debian derivatives, you can install lftp by running this command:

```
# apt-get install lftp
```

On Red Hat derivatives, you can install it by running this command:

```
# yum install lftp
```

If for some reason you need to install the lftp package from its source, you should use the following commands (be warned that when using some operating system versions, you may need to install other packages as well):

```
# ./configure --with-openssl=/usr/lib
# make; make install
```

If you have any SSL or TLS support issues, such as connections not initiating successfully, use the following command to check if the lftp utility has been compiled with the libgnutls or libssl functionality:

```
# ldd /usr/bin/lftp
```

In the resulting output, look for lines starting with either libgnutls or libssl to confirm if it has been compiled with this functionality. If you're not sure of the exact path of your lftp binary, simply run these commands to append to the ldd command above:

```
# updatedb; locate lftp
```

Getting Started

As is the case with old-style command-line FTP clients, you can either cram your connection commands onto one single line or enter a subshell of sorts and interact from there. The nslookup command offers a similar way of interacting with it.

First, an example of connecting directly to a remote host and only getting asked for a password:

```
# lftp chrisbinnie@secure.chrisftp.tld
Password:
```

In this example, I'm not entering a subshell yet; instead I'm passing the username on the command line directly. However, without doing that on one line, the output from lftp looks like this (minus the chrisbinnie@ element):

```
# lftp secure.chrisftp.tld
lftp secure.chrisftp.tld:-> user chrisbinnie
Password:
```

Note that I've added the user option to this interaction. Don't let the different ways of interfacing with the command confuse you. Occasionally, however one good reason to pay attention to this is that one of the world's largest web hosting companies seems to insist on using a username in this format on its shared hosting platform: chris@chris.binnie.tld. To my mind that's pretty nuts even though it's obvious why they prefer that format for tracking which host or domain name a user belongs to. Unless it's an e-mail address, however, using an @ sign within a username should probably be ruled illegal, punishable with a life sentence of working with Windows machines.

My objection to the username format is justified. To connect to one of the world's biggest web hosts, the resulting, confusing single-lined lftp connection looks like this:

```
# lftp chris@chris.binnie.tld@chris.binnie.tld
```

For clarity I'd probably suggest opting for the "user" subshell alternative, which I just looked at if you're forced to use weird usernames. Also, unlike common FTP file transfers, there are of course likely to be certificates involved if the connections are encrypted.

However, continuing on from the previous example and having entered my password, I receive a rather scary and unwelcome error after having tried to list files on the remote host with an ls command:

```
# ls
ls: Fatal error: Certificate verification: Not trusted
```

Incidentally if you encounter errors, type quit (don't press Ctrl+C).

When faced with such a problem, you can apply the following fix using your favorite text editor. You control your lftp preferences from within a resource file inside your home directory. By writing to a file called rc, as follows, you can add loads of different settings:

```
# mkdir /home/chrisbinnie/.lftp
# pico -w /home/chrisbinnie/.lftp/rc
set ssl:verify-certificate no
```

The first line creates a hidden directory in your home directory and the second fires up the pico editor; in this case to alter how SSL certificates are handled. Clearly this is not ideal because you're effectively ignoring the enforced certificate check. Bear in mind though that many FTP(S) servers will offer self-signed certificates as opposed to paying for a trusted certificate. This means that your credentials and commands sent during the connection will be difficult to eavesdrop on because they're encrypted, but the identity of the remote server won't be guaranteed. Still, there could be a server impersonating your file repository, with bad intentions, looking to steal your password. I stumbled across this nice fix for ignoring self-signed certificate errors, allowing you to use them seamlessly. This is explained well on this blog from Versatile Web Solutions: http://www.versatilewebsolutions.com/blog/2014/04/lftp-ftps-and-certificate-verification.html.

Here's what happens: Essentially you need to grab and store the certificate from the remote host that you'll be connecting to. You then refer to that certificate from within your lftp config. And, when you connect again in the future, you'll be able to tell if it's the same machine that you connected to last time.

To extract the certificate in question, you need a little assistance from OpenSSL. Using the built-in client known as s_client, you can manually establish a connection to a remote host (it will work with connections using SSL [Secure Sockets Layer] or its successor TLS [Transport Layer Security]).

OpenSSL suggests that the client it comes bundled with is only really intended for testing purposes and as a result it offers very basic interfacing. However, internally it does use much of the innards of the super-popular, all-pervasive OpenSSL ssl library, which is of comfort if you need to test fully.

Here's the OpenSSL command that the excellent web page suggests (replace your hostname before the :21 obviously):

```
# openssl s_client -showcerts -connect secure.chrisbinnie.tld:21 -starttls ftp
```

Having run that command you're presented with a flood of data that can be split into two parts. Figure 8-1 shows a purposely snipped certificate file (missing the "-----BEGIN CERTIFICATE-----" section heading at the top) presented at the top of the output. I've snipped the output to keep it brief. The part of this that you want to copy and paste into a file is this section (inclusive of the lines with the dashes at the beginning and the end).

```
VR0jBBgwFoAUR7MuiFgrCxnAkHmPglyGEx2aJEswDAYDVR0TBAUwAwEB/zANBgkq
hkiG9w0BAQsFAAOCAQEAOX/6phHgBhC5FxzY796gVjePocpnxMGEAxkbFWjvWsg3
Pu7F4KI5oYgWcYrd1pgLkFk/FqtNg8hE4e4dtmLICbEwrmEcdQa3m6c6WsV8YNtb
tgkDJCKxu4OUozAjDBDVb3+G+be7u3cVJhSdnIItGdM1e9ZqtVsaIN1Ii5wPcJXV
GXPDWtmzKvk2KvERWFcHCPR/prM8WX0cEpgsyvw37DT9FQzuJcs4jelrfqaV67wx
MXkYVRdkEennhtl9AvGexPZKHqAvr8YtdBFtFZ5AiEXF9lWTy/btxCVuJPjduSmo
p44Wd4384+UGv57+LH7v2CCSeZnpMgRJvQaMR41Lqw==
-----END CERTIFICATE-----
```

Figure 8-1. *An abbreviated certificate*

Figure 8-2 Shows a few more details of the connection, which confirms that it's a self-signed certificate.

```
TLS session ticket lifetime hint: 3600 (seconds)
TLS session ticket:
0000 - e2 29 0e 7f d2 6a 18 44-2e 0f 1f da c5 0f 09 80   .)...j.D........
0010 - ad 02 6a 2a 21 13 db 79-ed a6 20 fc 9d d9 5f 72   ..j*!..y.. ..._r
0020 - 31 f7 08 0d 7a 3c 7b dc-e3 a6 5e 1d f7 14 f5 ac   1...z<{...^.....
0030 - fd da 00 07 70 2f ee 98-2f 86 b4 c0 a8 01 d3 cc   ....p/../.......
0040 - ba 95 41 8e 27 4d 2a a2-4f 30 23 f4 f6 fb 93 b4   ..A.'M*.O0#.....
0050 - be 6a 24 e7 f2 7a 9b 30-7b 5c c7 c6 4d 6a e9 fc   .j$..z.O{\..Mj..
0060 - 50 2f 4c ed e9 02 79 f4-b9 6b de 93 81 a5 6f aa   P/L...y..k....o.
0070 - 53 11 2c e3 bf 72 45 4a-9d f9 43 b3 e2 11 70 56   S.,..rEJ..C...pV
0080 - db 8e bc e8 09 05 a1 ea-f6 9d a0 92 9b 7c 78 74   ............|xt
0090 - d0 ad 91 0e 0e 59 81 bc-30 ff 0c 40 45 97 24 70   .....Y..0..@E.$p

Start Time: 1441614757
Timeout    : 300 (sec)
Verify return code: 18 (self signed certificate)
```

Figure 8-2. *Some more information about the self-signed certificate and its connection*

After pasting the certificate information into a file (for example, I copied it into the /home/chrisbinnie/.lftp directory for ease), you can point your rc preference file at it. If you weren't using individual files (which are kept in a directory next to your main config), then you can choose not to create a directory and simply use a file called /home/yourname/.lftprc to keep your preferences config in if you want.

Let's follow the actions I took. First, paste your remote server's certificate into a file called `ftpbox-cert.crt` or similar:

```
# pico -w /home/chrisbinnie/.lftp/ftpbox-cert.crt
```

Next, look at your `/home/yourname/.lftp/rc` file and add the following line after removing the `verify` line you added initially:

```
set ssl:ca-file "ftpbox-cert.crt"
```

If you get another odd-looking error such as "`Certificate verification: certificate common name doesn't match requested hostname,`" then add this line to your `/home/yourname/.lftp/rc` file to ignore the hostname that was entered into the self-signed certificate:

```
set ssl:check-hostname no
```

Although you're potentially ignoring the hostname, you should see any changes to the certificate being presented to initialize the connection. This is obviously much better than blindly connecting to any old box that your DNS or network thinks is valid before you start uploading sensitive data.

The web page from Versatile Web Solutions that mentioned this trick also dutifully reminds us that even self-signed certificates expire, so be warned that you'll probably get nasty-looking errors when the remote certificate's expiration date is reached.

Alternatively, you can also connect to an anonymous FTP site that tacitly asks you to enter your e-mail address instead of a password, using the following command:

```
# lftp
# open -u anonymous,chris@binnie.tld -p 21 ftpbox.binnie.tld
```

If you want to set your anonymous password permanently, add this to your `rc` file (otherwise the username of the person using `lftp` will be used):

```
set ftp:anon-pass "chris@binnie.tld"
```

Main Configuration Options

You have the option, especially if you get stuck, of enabling the debugging option to your `rc` file: simply add the debug to switch it on. This is useful because otherwise `lftp` will run quietly in the background without much logging. If you want to output the complete debugging info then use this setting:

```
# debug 5
```

To make the logging less noisy, you have the option of this setting:

```
# debug 3
```

Incidentally this can be overridden by using the `-d` switch on the command line and the full debugging level will be displayed.

Let's look at just a sprinkling of the multitude of other options available to you now.

One option comes with a clearly defined caveat. I would highly suggest that you don't enable this, unless you absolutely have to, and only then for connecting to anonymous FTP sites. This is because lftp has the ability to bookmark FTP sites and include their passwords (which is highly insecure). It sounds like lftp is running a GUI (Graphical User Interface) when I mention that it offers bookmarks, but it's not. You can switch off the saving of passwords in your rc file like this:

```
set bmk:save-passwords no
```

Some FTP servers tend to be more finicky than others and they work incorrectly if "sync mode" isn't enabled. The so-called "sync mode" works by the lenient lftp patiently sending one command at a time and then waiting for a response. It can also help when a router is misbehaving a little.

If you don't enable sync mode, then lftp sends a whole bunch of commands in close succession and waits for a response. If it's used, you can potentially speed up the command exchanges. However; as I've stated, some hosts and routers don't approve of these floods of commands being sent, so by default "sync mode" is switched on to keep communications as sensible as possible.

If you're prudent, by tuning the lftp config settings, you can keep a look out for some servers and turn on "sync mode" if the banner, or title, includes a certain message. It's matched using regular expressions as shown here, where the pipe symbol acts as OR:

```
set ftp:auto-sync-mode "Rubbish Server|MS-based FTP Box"
```

In this example if the introductory welcome banner contains either "Rubbish Server" or "MS-based FTP Box", then "sync mode" will be automatically enabled while opening up the throttle for the other FTP sites that you connect to.

If you've used FTP to any extent, then you've almost certainly come across Passive Mode before. FTP, as a protocol, exclusively uses TCP (Transmission Control Protocol) (you want to know whether your upload made it after all) and avoids using UDP (User Datagram Protocol).

By default, FTP will attempt to use TCP port 21 to communicate over for its commands and TCP port 20 would be used for the actual payload (that is, the uploaded or downloaded data). However, all sorts of problems occur when port 20 isn't actually used for data transfers.

Apparently in Active Mode, an FTP client will look at one of the ephemeral ports (also known as non-privileged ports), which is higher than TCP ports 0 to 1023 for its data connection. In Active Mode, the ports are scrambled and some clients and servers tie themselves in knots. In Passive Mode (written as "PASV" in FTP as a command in case you get caught out by FTP parlance), you can sleep well at night knowing that TCP port 20 won't be used in the transactions but instead higher ephemeral port numbers will be. As a result good, old Passive Mode might save the day with firewalling rules or irritable routers.

You can always force PASV mode as follows within your rc file like so:

```
set ftp:passive-mode yes
```

If you're insistent on using Active Mode, you can force the PORT number. This is the TCP port that is used for the data connection, suggested by the client if PASV is not being used. To lock an active transfer to a specific IP address and port number, you can use these config settings:

```
set ftp:port-ipv4 123.123.123.123
```

```
set ftp:port-range 2000-3000
```

You can adjust 123.123.123.123 to your IP address and the second line lets you fine-tune your firewalled ports if need be.

To use SSL even on anonymous FTP servers so that your credentials or commands aren't exposed to the world at large, use this command:

```
set ftp:ssl-force yes
```

You can go one step further and also insist that all data be transferred over an encrypted connection, as follows:

```
set ftp:ssl-protect-data yes
```

That's a very sensible setting to my mind; unless it's public data, the slight transfer speed and CPU overhead is probably well worth it.

A common FTP command—used to refresh connections (if you type in the same way that I do) or check when an upload has completed—is the list or ls command (the dir command warrants a mention too). If you're keen to keep your connection as secure as possible, you probably also want to disguise the output that is produced by file listing. Try using this command in your rc file to manage that:

```
set ftp:ssl-protect-list yes
```

Sometimes the bandwidth on a connection that you're using is scarce or your FTP server software is ill-tempered. The flexible lftp has thought of everything and even lets you switch off the default QUIT command to politely close a connection. You can change the default like this:

```
set ftp:use-quit no
```

If you encounter an authoritative-looking user and password request over HTTP, you can use this option, changing username:password as you see fit:

```
set http:authorization "username:passwd"
```

Another option that I find useful is clobber, which lets you adjust your overwrite settings.

```
set xfer:clobber on
```

In this example, if clobber is turned off, the FTP GET commands won't overwrite existing files but instead will complain with an error message. On low-bandwidth links, you might want to test it as "off".

If you're taught anything as a fledgling techie, good housekeeping in any sysadmin's mind should include logging. You can keep a log of your transfers by pointing them at a file like this:

```
set xfer:log-file "/home/chrisbinnie/biglog.log"
```

I'm sure you'll agree that being able to retain all of your transfer details for future reference is a useful addition; it can be enabled and disabled whenever needed.

The Default lftp Config File

To give you a flavor of what the default configuration options look like, have a look at the config file.

Listing 8-1 shows the lftp config file, which resides at /etc/lftp.conf in its default state on Debian.

Listing 8-1. The Main Config File for lftp Found at /etc/lftp.conf

```
## some useful aliases
alias dir ls
alias less more
alias zless zmore
alias bzless bzmore
alias reconnect "close; cache flush; cd ."
alias edit "eval -f \"get $0 -o ~/.lftp/edit.tmp.$$ && shell \\\"cp -p ~/.lftp/edit.
tmp.$$ ~/.lftp/edit.tmp.$$.orig && $EDITOR ~/.lftp/edit.tmp.$$ && test ~/.lftp/edit.tmp.$$
-nt ~/.lftp/edit.tmp.$$.orig\\\" && put ~/.lftp/edit.tmp.$$ -o $0; shell rm -f ~/.lftp/edit.
tmp.$$*\""


## make prompt look better
set prompt "lftp \S\? \u\@\h:\w> "
## some may prefer colors (contributed by Matthew <mwormald@optusnet.com.au>)
#set prompt "\[\e[1;30m\]\[\[\e[0;34m\]f\[\e[1m\]t\[\e[37m\]p\[\e[30m\]] \[\e[34m\]\u\
[\e[0;34m\]\@\[\e[1m\]\h\[\e[1;30m\]:\[\e[1;34m\]\w\[\e[1;30m\]>\[\e[0m\] "
## Uncomment the following two lines to make switch cls and ls, making
## cls the default.
#alias ls command cls
#alias hostls command ls


## default protocol selection
#set default-protocol/ftp.*      ftp
#set default-protocol/www.*      http
#set default-protocol/localhost file


## this makes lftp faster but doesn't work with some sites/routers
#set ftp:sync-mode off


## synchronous mode for broken servers and/or routers
set sync-mode/ftp.idsoftware.com on
set sync-mode/ftp.microsoft.com on
set sync-mode/sunsolve.sun.com on
## extended regex to match first server message for automatic sync-mode.
set auto-sync-mode "Microsoft FTP Service|MadGoat|MikroTik"


## if default ftp passive mode does not work, try this:
# set ftp:passive-mode off


## Set this to follow http redirections
set xfer:max-redirections 10
```

```
## Proxy can help to pass a firewall
## Environment variables ftp_proxy, http_proxy and no_proxy are used to
## initialize the below variables automatically. You can set them here too.
##
## ftp:proxy must communicate with client over ftp protocol, squid won't do.
## This can be e.g. TIS-FWTK or rftpd. User and password are optional.
# set ftp:proxy ftp://[user:pass@]your_ftp_proxy:port
## ...but squid still can be used to access ftp servers, using hftp protocol:
# set ftp:proxy http://your.squid.address:port
## ...if squid allows CONNECT to arbitrary ports, then you can use CONNECT
## instead of hftp:
# set ftp:use-hftp no
##
## no proxy for host
# set ftp:proxy/local_host ""
## or domain
# set ftp:proxy/*.domain.com ...
##
## http:proxy must communicate with client over http protocol, e.g. squid.
## Default port is 3128.
# set http:proxy your_http_proxy[:port]
## hftp:proxy must also be an http proxy. It is used for FTP over HTTP access.
# set hftp:proxy your_http_proxy[:port]
##
## net:no-proxy disables proxy usage for list of domains.
# set net:no-proxy .domain.com,.otherdom.net

## If you don't have direct ftp access, this setting can be useful to select
## hftp instead of ftp automatically.
# set ftp:proxy http://your.http.proxy:port

## This can be used for automatic saving of configuration
# set at-exit "set > ~/.lftp/settings"
# source ~/.lftp/settings

## and this is for remembering last site
## (combine with previous rule if you want)
# set at-exit "bo a last"
# open last

## Terminal strings to set titlebars for terminals that don't
## properly specify tsl and fsl capabilities.
## Use cmd:set-term-status to enable this.
set cmd:term-status/*screen* "\e_\T\e\\"
set cmd:term-status/*xterm* "\e[11;0]\e]2;\T\007\e[11]"
set cmd:term-status/*rxvt* "\e[11;0]\e]2;\T\007\e[11]"
# set cmd:set-term-status on
```

```
## If you don't like advertising lftp or servers hate it, set this:
# set ftp:anon-pass "mozilla@"
# set ftp:client ""
# set http:user-agent "Mozilla/4.7 [en] (WinNT; I)"

# try inet6 before inet
set dns:order "inet6 inet"
```

The top section talks about aliases and what equals what (for example, on Windows that dir is the near-equivalent to the Unix-type ls command for all intents and purposes). The second section in Listing 8-1 is about altering the prompt to your preference. The third section asks about setting a default HTTP (The Hypertext Transfer Protocol) or FTP protocol to connect to. The third entry in that section is set default-protocol/localhost file, which is only used if you drop into a subshell after launching lftp and then type open and a server name. The default is FTP. I have already covered "sync mode" and PASV; the redirections that are mentioned were added for HTTP connections mainly and prevent the client from being redirected from one page or site to another, which some web browsers can be subject to with some web sites.

The fourth section shown in Listing 8-1 shows that lftp can also handle pushing and pulling traffic via a proxy. I'll leave you to explore these options. Have a look at the following settings:

```
set at-exit "set > ~/.lftp/settings"
source ~/.lftp/settings
```

By uncommenting those lines, you can ask lftp to write your current config automatically to the file /home/yourname/.lftp/settings when exiting the program. Then when you launch the software you'll be able to retrieve those settings with the source command on the second line.

Finally, if you want your previous connection details remembered (because they're a pain to type for example), then uncomment these two lines:

```
set at-exit "bo a last"
open last
```

Similar to the previous set at-exit setting, if you enable this setting, then lftp will save and open the last server that you were connected to.

Adding Multiple Options to One Line

Note also that you don't have to keep tweaking your config or rc file. If you want to test settings that you plan to write to your config file later, or just use an unusual combination to talk to a specific server, then lftp is equally accommodating on the command line. The following example throws one-off config settings in the direction of lftp by using the -e option:

```
# lftp -e "set ftp:ssl-allow off;" -u chrisbinnie,passwd ftpbox.chrisbinnie.tld
```

You can chain these config settings and separate them individually with a semicolon.

Mirroring Directories

You can use lftp to mirror a local and remote directory with relative ease by running the mirror command at the lftp prompt. Make sure that you are in the correct directories first, both on your local and remote machines. If you use the mirror command with its -c option so that the transfer will continue if interrupted, you can copy all of the contents from the remote directory to your local directory.

```
# mirror -c
```

You should be presented with a suitable amount of transaction details once the transfer has finished. This will be information relating to the number of copied directories, files, and symlinks and those that were removed. As you'd expect, there will also be bandwidth and transfer time statistics to keep you right when scripting any content syncing. Clearly, this easy command allows you to solve issues that arise under a few different circumstances. For example, you could employ this option for backing up a web site or syncing data between a cluster of web servers.

Using Regular Expressions

Of course, you can also use regex with lftp transfers. Here is a simple example from the command line for uploading files:

```
# lftp -e 'mirror -R -i "\.(php|html)$" /path_on_localmachine/ /' -u chrisbinnie,passwd
ftpbox.chrisbinnie.tld
```

With the username chrisbinnie and the simple password passwd, you connect to the server ftpbox. chrisbinnie.tld. As you can see, I'm also using the mirror command (with the -R option for coping everything recursively); the lftp will only upload php and html files. That's a very handy option to have available for scripting.

Troubleshooting Tips

If you ever get stale file listings and can't quite fathom why, this will clear current listings suitably from the lftp prompt:

```
> cache flush
```

If you're interested in looking further into clearing stale file caching then, again from the lftp prompt, type:

```
> help cache
```

You should see expiration times and memory size limit options and see how to change them. This can be handy if your file names and directories get written to or deleted on a frequent basis.

Summary

It goes without saying that the Internet is no longer the nice place it once was. There's little hope of returning to your system having left it unprotected for any length of time and finding it in the same state. On today's Internet, it's important to encrypt the data that you transmit. That applies to the data flow and the entering and acceptance of credentials.

This chapter covered but a few useful lftp features. For more options, skim the lftp manual and search online for some of the problematic scenarios that other users have found a solution for by using lftp. The lftp utility is brimming with features and as long as you take care that the login credentials are no longer sent in clear text then your data is pretty safe. Thanks to lftp you have a good chance of being able to run encrypted FTP sessions successfully even without an SSH server being present at the other end.

■ ■ ■

## CHAPTER 9

Making the Most of the Screen Utility

The "screen" utility is the tool that every sysadmin should not be able to live without. It allows you to put your SSH session on hold and return to it whenever you like, from anywhere. It's widely supported across the Unix-type flavors and thankfully it is really simple to get working despite its more advanced aspects, which admittedly encourage eye-strain. This chapter provides a refresher on some of the screen utility's excellent functionality.

Screen Utility Basics

For clarity, I'll be focusing on Linux; however, the differences between distributions should be largely negligible. Chances are the screen utility is already installed, but if not, use the following commands.

On Debian derivatives, use this command:

```
# apt-get install screen
```

On Red Hat derivatives, use this command:

```
# yum install screen
```

To launch the utility, enter:

```
# screen
```

This creates a pseudo-shell session.

To exit from the screen (and save your existing work), press Ctrl+a d.

■ **Note**   In general, think of pressing Ctrl+a (aka the "escape key") as your main way of manipulating the screen utility. Pressing the *d* key, which stands for "detach," leaves that console session as detached (and running in the background). When your command has stopped running, the screen utility will kill the window that it ran in. If the window in question was the visible (foreground) window, then your display will be pushed toward the previous window. If no window is available at all, then the screen utility will quit.

To exit from (or quit) the shell completely, press Ctrl+d; exactly in the same way you would exit from a login session. Be warned, though, that all the work you've done during that session will be lost when you see the following response:

```
[screen is terminating]
```

Using the Screen Utility—A Simple Example

To make things easy, I'll start with a simple scenario: using one screen window. First log in to your remote SSH server, using your SSH client, and then type the following:

```
# screen
```

To leave a command running and then return to it after closing an SSH session, use the top command:

```
# top
```

To detach from that session, press Ctrl+a d. To jump back to your saved, background session, type this:

```
# screen -r
```

The -r simply means "reattach," or I think of it as standing for "resume". If there's only one detached session then that's it. Simple, huh? Press Ctrl+a d and then type screen -r a few times to get used to it.

Listing Sessions

If you're dealing with multiple sessions, you could do worse than to label them with descriptive names. To see whether you have multiple sessions running, you can use the ls command:

```
# screen -ls
```

If you have multiple sessions running, the output will look similar to the one shown in Listing 9-1.

Listing 9-1. A List of Multiple Sessions

```
There are screens on:
 26075.pts-0.chrisbinniehost    (Detached)
       26056.pts-0.chrisbinniehost    (Detached)
       25700.pts-0.chrisbinniehost    (Detached)
3 Sockets in /var/run/screen/S-chrisbinnie.
```

To reattach your current view to one of the multiple sessions, all you have to do is look at its unique session number and enter a command like this one:

```
# screen -r 26075
```

Remember that you can resume your session from any computer, anywhere (assuming you have SSH access, of course).

If you are juggling multiple sessions and possibly many SSH windows (whether they be "PuTTY"- or "xterm"-based), then you probably need a way of managing them. It's easy for the best of us to get lost with similar-looking terminals running near-identical commands. In order to rename your current SSH window's title, press Ctrl+a A (that is: Ctrl+a Shift+a). At the bottom of the current window, you should get a prompt to allow you to rename your session if that went to plan. Figure 9-1 shows what should happen if that's the case.

```
top - 10:21:03 up 62 days, 19:29,  3 users,  load average: 0.00, 0.00, 0.00
Tasks: 150 total,   1 running, 149 sleeping,   0 stopped,   0 zombie
Cpu0  :  0.0%us,  1.0%sy,  0.0%ni, 99.0%id,  0.0%wa,  0.0%hi,  0.0%si,  0.0%st
Cpu1  :  0.0%us,  1.0%sy,  0.0%ni, 99.0%id,  0.0%wa,  0.0%hi,  0.0%si,  0.0%st
Mem:   3924628k total,  1712364k used,  2212264k free,   545784k buffers
Swap:  4620284k total,     404k used,  4619880k free,   482492k cached

  PID USER      PR  NI  VIRT  RES  SHR S %CPU %MEM    TIME+  COMMAND
26071 d609288   20   0 25916 1436 1064 S  2.0  0.0   0:22.34 top
    1 root      20   0 21436 1396 1156 S  0.0  0.0   0:04.62 /sbin/init
    2 root      20   0     0    0    0 S  0.0  0.0   0:02.98 [kthreadd]
    3 root      RT   0     0    0    0 S  0.0  0.0   0:01.14 [migration/0]
    4 root      20   0     0    0    0 S  0.0  0.0   0:22.49 [ksoftirqd/0]
    5 root      RT   0     0    0    0 S  0.0  0.0   0:00.00 [stopper/0]
    6 root      RT   0     0    0    0 S  0.0  0.0   0:20.31 [watchdog/0]
    7 root      RT   0     0    0    0 S  0.0  0.0   0:00.92 [migration/1]
    8 root      RT   0     0    0    0 S  0.0  0.0   0:00.00 [stopper/1]
    9 root      20   0     0    0    0 S  0.0  0.0   0:20.04 [ksoftirqd/1]




Set window's title to: chris-screen-window-numero-uno
```

Figure 9-1. *You can see how to rename the current session name*

Figure 9-2 shows that my "PuTTY" window title has been suitably changed as a result. This should help avoid any potential mishaps of pressing the Enter key in the wrong terminal when logged in as the root user.

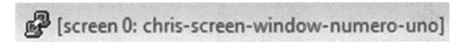

Figure 9-2. *Change the current SSH window title for safety*

Of course, it would be much more convenient to connect to each session using a name and not a session number. It's simple to do.

1. When you launch a new session, instead of just typing "screen," you can type:

    ```
    # screen -S chrisbinnie-linux
    ```

    Where `chrisbinnie-linux` is your screen name.

2. Then when you use the `screen -ls` command again, you'll see something like this among your other session names:

    ```
    26791.chrisbinnie-linux       (Detached)
    ```

3. Finally, to reconnect to that screen, you can forget the 26971 session number and instead use the session name, like this:

    ```
    # screen -r chrisbinnie-linux
    ```

Now that you have some of the basics under your belt, it's time to try a few of the other features included with the superhero screen utility.

Some Useful Tips and Commands

This sections covers some tips and commands that may come in handy, depending on your needs.

Attaching an Existing Session to Your Current Window

If you've left a session attached and need to detach it in order to attach it to your current window, you can use the following command followed by your screen session name. For example:

```
# screen -dRR chrisbinnie-linux
```

You start by attaching to an existing session and if you (or someone else) have already attached to it elsewhere, the command detaches the session from the other display. If no session exists with such a name, then it creates one for you. Note that if multiple sessions are found, the screen utility will use the first one by default. The first R means "reattach" a session but create it if required; the second R adds the option to use the first session if there's more than one.

Using Passwords

You might want to detach from your screen utility's session and then reattach from a shared computer. To force your session to become password protected (with your login password), you can use this clever little keystroke combination (like many other options) from inside your session:

```
Ctrl+a x
```

Killing a Session

You are certain to want to close down your sessions. Once attached to a session, you can issue this keystroke combo:

```
Ctrl+a k
```

And as a result, at the bottom of the window, you are prompted with this sensible question:

```
Really kill this window [y/n]
```

Choose wisely.

Logging Your Session

The screen utility provides a couple of options to log what your session is doing when you're absent. One option, called command mode, allows you to dump the data to a file. Here's how: Press the escape key, which is Ctrl+a followed by a colon (:), to open a prompt at the bottom of the window. Then type this, for example:

```
hardcopy -h chris-file-dump
```

This places a file called chris-file-dump on the filesystem that contains the output from your session.

You can also use variations of the hardcopy command—for example, hardcopy_append or hardcopydir. The hardcopy_append command, if set to on. means that screen appends the files created. Otherwise, these files are overwritten each time. The hardcopydir command changes which directory you want to dump your log files into, and the former adds to an existing dump file as opposed to creating a new one.

The other logging option available to you is grabbing any output and dumping it to a log file. By default, this file is called screenlog.N, where N is your screen session number. To get this working, you can use the following at start time using the -L switch:

```
# screen -L
```

Type something to generate output (like the ls command or similar) to add to the log file. Be warned, however, that you're not necessarily going to be able to read every log file with total clarity. This is because your favorite text editors and viewers might potentially treat it like a binary file, thanks to some special characters. For example, you might receive a response with the familiar error: "screenlog.0" may be a binary file. See it anyway?".

Even if that error does rear its head, you can see from the output of the following file command (to check the file type) that the screenlog.0 file is indeed a straightforward text file.

```
# file screenlog.0
screenlog.0: ASCII text, with CRLF line terminators, with escape sequences
```

Finally, you can also achieve the same logging functionality from within the terminal, if you forget to launch your session with the -L option, by using this key combination:

```
Ctrl+a H
```

Saving Config Settings to Your Home Directory

The screen utility also allows you to distinctly apply individual config settings to your username by saving them to a file in your home directory, called .screenrc. For instance, with the following instructions I am changing the default logfile name (remember screenlog.N?). Then, so that I can follow the logfile by using the tail command, I decide to "flush" the session's output to the file every second.

```
deflog on
logfile   /home/chrisbinnie/chris-screen-logfile
logfile flush 1
```

You can change many, many, many other things in your .screenrc file. You could add the following bindings, for example, to change movement between your screen sessions:

```
bind ',' prev
bind '.' next
```

To find out about all the key binding once you're inside a screen session, type CTRL-a?.

Even if you're brimming with chutzpah I heartily recommend that you don't use your favorite online search device to look for "screen hardstatus". Think along the lines of taskbars! I will say no more and remain cryptic. For those with questionable sanity amongst us, here is a nicely-written piece with more information: http://www.kilobitspersecond.com/2014/02/10/understanding-gnu-screens-hardstatus-strings/.

Running a Command in a Script

Note that the screen utility also plays very nicely when being run inside scripts. For example, you might run something like this inside a script:

```
# screen -S PingWWW -d -m ping web.chrisbinnie.tld
```

Here, I simply launch a session called "PingWWW" and use it to launch the ping command to check if a host is responding. The possibilities are endless, as you can imagine. With the screen utility, you can safely assume that the binary executable or the shell script that you launch will continue running in an open session. Try it for yourself.

Tricksy Telnet

Here is an application of the screen utility that I really like. Picture this: You don't have access to a Telnet client on your workstation and you need to connect to a networking switch that doesn't have SSH access available. As it's a LAN-to-LAN connection you're not entirely concerned about exposing your login credentials over Telnet (it's a small LAN and you're traversing a single switch, which means there's less chance of packet sniffing taking place successfully). Why bother hunting for a specific Telnet client when you can use the screen utility? Here is how to do it with the screen utility:

```
# screen //telnet switch.chrisbinnie.tld 23
```

You can also try typing a GET / to a webserver in order to receive HTML back:

```
# screen //telnet www.chrisbinnie.tld 80
GET /

<HTML>
<HEAD><TITLE> ...
```

This is an abbreviated example of the start of the HTML output that you would see.

■ **Note**   The screen utility's manual is lengthy. For a quick reference, type man screen at a prompt. For some useful web-based versions of the exceptional manual, refer to http://www.gnu.org/software/screen/manual/screen.html.

Summary

It's safe to say that I have barely scratched the surface of the screen utility. Every time that I use it I'm almost certain to discover another feature that I should commit to memory. It's difficult to argue against using the screen utility for all sorts of tasks. And the nice thing is that you might only need to remember two commands to get a great deal of its functionality working for you: Ctrl+a d to detach and then screen -r to reattach once you've logged back in. Hopefully having read this refresher of (or indeed introduction to) the screen utility, you can put your knowledge to good use and avoid tearing your hair out the next time that a console fails to realize that you were still using it.

CHAPTER 10

■ ■ ■

Improve Security with SELinux

If you need a secure solution for your Linux system, then SELinux may be just right for you. SELinux can be referred to as an implementation of the FLASK security architecture. FLASK (Flux Advanced Security Kernel) is aimed at securing operating systems and is a joint venture between the National Security Agency (NSA) in the United States, NAI Labs, the Security Computing Cooperation and the MITRE Corporation. Rather than rely on DAC (Discretionary Access Control), SELinux provides a sturdy mechanism for which to enforce Mandatory Access Controls (MAC) to improve security.

This chapter provides an introduction to SELinux's concepts and operating methods, offering a broad overview of the relevant configs that work with Red Hat derivatives.

Understanding Key Concepts

The concepts and rules should apply to other Linux distributions. If they don't work for you directly, use an online search to look for the correct path or package name.

Deny Everything, Everything

Every good sysadmin will be familiar with the "default deny" approach to security. Imagine trying to enter a private members club for a function without being a member; without being explicitly added to the guest list, you're simply not allowed in. Apply that methodology to security and you'll soon see that such an approach is the only serious way to deploy security practices. The NSA-conceived package does exactly that and refers to it as least-privilege (in its "strict" policy).

Conversely, SELinux realizes, from a human standpoint, that anything too strict within its configs will result in sysadmins simply disabling SELinux.

If issues with applications and SELinux appear impossible to fix on a production system, sometimes the pressure on sysadmins to restore functionality is too great and security might need to take a back seat until testing has been completed. As a result, SELinux cleverly attempts to provide a number of modular policies to help assist.

By design, SELinux works with caution in mind. For example, the "targeted" policy deals with carefully selected system processes, hopefully battle-hardened. In CentOS 4, in the region of only 15 added targets were included in the package (such as the very popular HTTPD and named daemons), but in CentOS 5 there were over 200 targets included and more recently almost all services are covered.

It's a sensible approach because false positives are more damaging than you might at first think. One common way of eluding safeguards, such as with a security officer protecting a museum's precious objet d'art, is to pester a security officer by triggering a sufficient number of alarms. Eventually he decides that the alarm system is broken. Ultimately, he either switches off the alarm or continues to simply ignores it when it rings.

91

■ **Note** There's a running joke among sysadmins about not learning SELinux to any degree, panicking, and just switching it off. The joke goes that someone involved heavily in the project, Dan Walsh, actually weeps (and, according to some, a kitten also dies) whenever someone uses the command `setenforce 0` to switch off SELinux!

There's more here on a dedicated site: `http://stopdisablingselinux.com`.

Segregating Applications

The basic premise of how SELinux is designed isn't a difficult concept to master: SELinux's aim is one of separation. By that I mean rather than trusting applications on your server to never be compromised and always behave exactly as you would expect, SELinux fears the worst.

In simple terms, SELinux will insist that an application can't go wandering off around your filesystem and write to just any old file or indeed spawn any process. This is a highly effective way to help mitigate the impact from attacks and mistakes. These attacks and issues might include buffer overflows and clumsy typos in config files. In some cases, this approach can completely remove potentially catastrophic consequences, meaning that a compromise only affects a tiny attack surface. By segregating your applications with different access rules, essentially the MACs I mentioned in the introduction, SELinux renders the infectious habits of badly behaving applications impotent. In relation to Unix-type architecture, it goes against the grain. Somewhat surprisingly, SELinux apparently has little concept of a "root" superuser, the omnipotent user, and also ignores the `setuid` and `setgid` binaries.

Some Key Characteristics

Let's spend a moment considering some of SELinux's main attributes.

Thankfully, because SELinux first surfaced in 1998 and has reached a high level of maturity, you are unlikely to discover any massive stumbling blocks by using your distro's package manager to install it. The patching of an errant application can still be challenging when it breaks SELinux rules, however.

According to the NSA (`http://www.nsa.gov`), some of the key characteristics of Security Enhanced Linux are as follows:

- Clean separation of policy from enforcement

- Well-defined policy interfaces

- Individual labels and controls for kernel objects and services

- Caching of access decisions for efficiency

- Support for policy changes

- Ability to control process initialization, inheritance, and program execution

- Different filesystems, directories, files, and open file description controls

- Power to manipulate sockets, messages, and network interfaces

In terms of distribution support, SELinux has been available since Red Hat Enterprise Linux (RHEL) version 4 and this support, as you'd quite rightly expect, is directly passed on to its offspring in both CentOS and Scientific Linux. Note, however, that from the RHEL4 version and thereafter, SELinux has aimed to provide further compatibility and now is bundled with friendlier configs as opposed to a more restrictive, government-spy configuration.

Understanding Domains and How They Can Be Used

Although *domains* aren't used often, it helps to know that they exist. There isn't actually a difference between a domain and a "type"; domains are sometimes used to refer to the type of a process.

With segmenting applications in mind, consider a scenario where system users in the guest_t and xguest_t domains can't execute applications in their home directories, but users in the user_t and staff_t domains can.

In order to allow users in the guest_t domain to launch some required content in the user home directories, you can use this command:

```
# /usr/sbin/setsebool -P allow_guest_exec_content on
```

To reverse that, simply do this:

```
# /usr/sbin/setsebool -P allow_guest_exec_content off
```

Incidentally, the -P option can be removed if you do not want the changes to remain after a reboot.

Setting Up SELinux

While most Linux distributions will allow you to set up SELinux from a fresh installation, in this section let's consider how to install it on an existing server.

Installation On Existing Servers

This task is probably far more sensible to practice on a virtual machine or test box. On an existing server, the way to do this is to set up warnings only, using permissive mode (in case your system falls over or it fails to boot after setting it live, which is easy to achieve). By doing this before enabling "enforcing" mode, you will increase your chances of success. Let's look at how to do that in the following sections.

Packages Required for Install

The packages that Red Hat derivatives require (depending on which functionality you require) can usually be covered with this command:

```
# yum install selinux-policy selinux-policy-targeted libselinux-utils policycoreutils
policycoreutils-python mcstrans setroubleshoot-server setools setools-console
```

Any packages that are already installed should simply be updated.

Changing Modes and Policies

The next thing to do is set permissive mode, which you will do now.

When deploying SELinux, you can opt for either of two prebuilt policies: the fully restrictive approach (the "strict" policy) or the targeted policy.

The targeted policy is more forgiving in the sense that it targets key applications that are most likely to be generically used by a sysadmin. In this case, everything else on your system uses the unconfined domain (which means it's not monitored by SELinux; more on this shortly). Listing 10-1 shows some descriptions of the options available in the config file /etc/selinux/config. Note the modes at the top and then the policies.

Listing 10-1. A Key SELinux Config File Found at /etc/selinux/config

```
# This file controls the state of SELinux on the system.
# SELINUX= can take one of these three values:
# enforcing - SELinux security policy is enforced.
# permissive - SELinux prints warnings instead of enforcing.
# disabled - SELinux is fully disabled.
SELINUX=permissive
# SELINUXTYPE= type of policy in use. Possible values are:
# targeted - Only targeted network daemons are protected.
# strict - Full SELinux protection.
SELINUXTYPE=targeted
# SETLOCALDEFS= Check local definition changes
SETLOCALDEFS=0
```

The comments in the /etc/selinux/config file indicate that enforcing is strict and permissive is much more relaxed. "Permissive" mode means SELinux just warns about issues (in a fresh installation that might be many). As we've said, thankfully you can use permissive mode for debugging issues without breaking your system. Needless to say, only the brave will go directly for the strict policy.

Under normal circumstances, at this stage you can simply make sure that your config file has SELINUX=permissive and SELINUXTYPE=targeted.

Activating SELinux

Next, in order to set SELinux live, you now use this command:

```
# selinux-activate
```

SELinux will attempt to label all the files on your drives with a sensible group name. With large disks, this will take a very long time.

Once completed you can expect a reboot. Then, after the system is back up, run the following command:

```
# check-selinux-installation
```

Now for one penultimate adjustment, edit the file /etc/grub.conf to activate auditing and then reboot using the following command:

```
# vi /etc/grub.conf
```

Add the audit=1 option to the kernel boot line to enable kernel auditing. This should assist by introducing verbose logging. Remove this setting once you are happy with your build, if you wish to cut down on logging. Now reboot the machine as so:

```
# reboot
```

Post-Install Tools

You will see tools such as checkpolicy, possibly policycoreutils, and selinux-basics. The prebuilt policies (called strict and targeted) will look through anything that you have installed.

These policies are hopefully clever enough to help SELinux apply the correct policy modules. If you're faced with lots of unwanted errors or if you want to tune the policy to suit your needs perfectly, then you can install the policy sources package selinux-policy-src. You can also create your own policy modules without installing the source for the majority of policies.

Operating SELinux

Let's move on to the more operational aspects of SELinux now. To start off, consider how you can tell which SELinux settings are currently enabled.

Current Status

For a quick check on which policy and mode is being used on a server currently, you can use the sestatus command to query your system settings. Note that the "Mode from Config File" setting is used after a reboot, as opposed to the one temporarily set live on the system in "Current Mode," as shown in Listing 10-2.

Listing 10-2. The SELinux Status Via the Command Line

```
SELinux status: enabled
SELinuxfs mount: /selinux
Current mode: permissive
Mode from config file: enforcing
Policy version: 21
Policy from config file: targeted
```

If you want to permanently apply changes to the policy settings, then altering the /etc/selinux/config file will mean that they will survive reboots.

To check which mode is currently being used, simply run this command:

```
# getenforce
```

Contexts

Now we will look at "contexts". In SELinux, contexts are applied to a number of system components such as directories and files or processes, for example. We'll look at adjusting contexts in a moment.

Before then have a quick look at the manual for the ls command, by typing man ls to see the -Z option. This switch stands for -context and displays any associated security context of files on the filesystem.

The output from a command that includes a –Z option will display mode, user, group, and security context. That's all contexts are, to all intents and purposes, they are a record of the associated security in place by SELinux for a particular component. Additionally, you can conveniently add the -Z option to a few other utilities such as the ps command. For example, you can see all sorts of extra information for each file, such as the /etc/hosts file shown:

```
# ls -alZ /etc/hosts
-rw-r--r-- root root system_u:object_r:etc_t:s0 /etc/hosts
```

Compare the output above to the example below. You also can see the differences between the root system object and the files in my home directory:

```
# ls -Z chrisbinnie.sh
-rw-r--r-- chris users user_u:object_r:user_home_t:s0 chrisbinnie.sh
```

And similarly, the process table reports the following when using the ps command and -Z as below (bear in mind my mention of the unconfined domain earlier):

```
# ps -efZ |grep ssh
system_u:system_r:unconfined_t:s0-s0:c0.c1023 root 7323 19329 0 12:12 ? 00:00:00 sshd:
chris [priv]
system_u:system_r:unconfined_t:s0-s0:c0.c1023 chris 7329 7323 0 12:12 ? 00:00:00 sshd:
chris@pts/0
system_u:system_r:unconfined_t:s0-s0:c0.c1023 root 9176 19329 0 11:11 ? 00:00:00 sshd:
chris [priv]
system_u:system_r:unconfined_t:s0-s0:c0.c1023 chris 9220 9176 0 11:11 ? 00:00:01 sshd:
chris@pts/1
system_u:system_r:unconfined_t:s0-s0:c0.c1023 root 19329 1 0 Dec22 ? 00:10:10 /usr/sbin/sshd
system_u:system_r:unconfined_t:s0-s0:c0.c1023 root 24249 19329 0 13:16 ? 00:10:10 sshd:
chris [priv]
system_u:system_r:unconfined_t:s0-s0:c0.c1023 chris 24255 24249 0 13:13 ? 00:00:00 sshd:
chris@pts/2
```

This output hopefully makes sense. You can see that the premise behind the segregation is actually very simple in the sense that access is only allowed between similar SELinux types. In other words, the user chris cannot write to the domain belonging to the system and, along the same vein, only user_u access is granted to use those in that domain.

Administrating SELinux

What about a relatively common issue that you might face? Namely, having the ability to alter individual files directly. Think of a shell script that you've written and want to execute, as an example.

Among other tools, the semanage fcontext command will achieve this and change the context in SELinux. However, you need to be aware that any changes you make do not stay in place after either relabeling the filesystem or if you run the restorecon command to put configs back in place. Getting the file type wrong is a frequent source of frustration and causes SELinux to deny access and trigger denials.

Using the chcon command to make temporary changes to contexts is reasonably easy. Let's look at changing the type of a file called new_httpd.conf:

```
# semanage fcontext -t httpd_sys_content_t new_httpd.conf
```

To change a directory (httpd_files in this case) and its contents in the same way you might use something like this:

```
# semanage fcontext -a -t httpd_sys_content_t "/httpd_files(/.*)?"
```

Note that this also affects all the directory's contents. Checking the changes that you've made can be as simple as this for a file:

```
# ls -lZ new_httpd.conf
```

And similarly, like this for a directory:

```
# ls -dZ httpd_files
```

If all else fails, you can restore contexts as alluded to earlier.

```
# /sbin/restorecon -R -v /etc/apache2/tmp
```

If you're faced with mounting a new filesystem and aren't declaring a policy immediately, you can mount a filesystem like this, using the following syntax:

```
# mount -o context=SELinux_user:role:type:level
```

In this case, if you wanted to make any changes persistent, modify the file /etc/fstab. This example is for a persistent NFS mount (Network File System), which adds a new entry as so:

```
-> server:/export /local/mount/ nfs context="system_u:object_r:httpd_sys_content_t:s0" 0 0
```

If you want to retain contexts when you're copying files, use this command option for cp as follows:

```
# cp --preserve=context chris_file binnie_file
```

If you want to add new users, run something like this:

```
# /usr/sbin/useradd -Z user_u chrisbinnie
```

Without the --preserve=context option being used, SELinux uses a different context. If you copied a file called testcopy into the /tmp directory, you might see something like this by running ls -Z:

```
-rw-r--r--. root root unconfined_u:object_r:user_tmp_t:s0 /tmp/testcopy
```

Making Context Changes Persistent

To make SELinux context changes persist permanently, you can use the following options:

```
# /usr/sbin/semanage fcontext -a options file-name/directory
```

An example of how this might look is:

```
# semanage fcontext -a -t samba_share_t /home/chris/script
```

The first switch -a will add a new record, whereas as you've guessed, passing -t defines a type (samba_share_t, in this case).

A caveat is that you need to use the full path to the file or directory. To make these changes permanent, you need to apply them as so:

```
# /sbin/restorecon -v file-name/directory
```

That command writes your config to a contexts file on the filesystem such as:

```
/etc/selinux/targeted/contexts/files/file_contexts.
```

Verifying Labels

If you're struggling with debugging MAC rules, then you should start with looking at *labeling*. This is because if an application has been assigned the wrong label, then its process might not work as expected.

A common cause for such a problem is when a non-standard directory, such as /etc/apache/tmp, is used.

Getting the context wrong is also easy. You can use a tool to help out with this issue, which you can find at /usr/sbin/matchpathcon. This tool will try to compare the context of a file path with the default label for that path and then either report mismatches or respond with "verified". Of course, you can always turn to the restorecon command to fix any issues if required and put written-to-disk rules back in place.

Another command that fills your screen with useful config info is /usr/sbin/getsebool. A sample of its output is as follows:

```
allow_console_login --> off
allow_cvs_read_shadow --> off
allow_daemons_dump_core --> on
allow_daemons_use_tty --> on
allow_domain_fd_use --> on
allow_execheap --> off
allow_execmem --> on
allow_execmod --> off
allow_execstack --> on
```

If you grep for a service, you can adjust the settings with this command:

```
# /usr/sbin/setsebool -P allow_httpd_anon_write on
```

Again as we used it in the same way earlier, -P is used as persistence.

Watch out because there's also a potential issue for port numbers. A rogue service attempting to open unusual ports will trigger SELinux denials. You can list the assigned ports per application as follows:

```
# /usr/sbin/semanage port -l
```

The potential issue is that you might get a "cannot bind to address" error from the application itself at boot time if SELinux steps in at this stage.

If you want to add config, in order to allow a port for the HTTPD daemon to use, for example, just run this command with the -a switch:

```
# /usr/sbin/semanage port -a -t http_port_t -p tcp 8100
```

I'm sure you get the idea of how this applies to other ports.

Daemons

For stopping and starting your daemons, you can use the usual methods on Red Hat derivatives.

Other operating systems might differ a little; check if you need to prepend `run_init` as follows if you're using a distribution that predates the use of `systemd`:

```
# run_init /etc/init.d/httpd start
```

The `run_init` command helps to run an init script with the proper SELinux context. This prompts for a password and uses the config within the file `/etc/selinux/POLICYTYPE/contexts/initrc_context`. An example might be `/etc/selinux/targeted/contexts/initrc_context` for the targeted policy.

Troubleshooting

You will likely face issues that take time to resolve as you learn your way. Thankfully, there are lots of routes to explore and tools to assist you if you need to resolve issues.

Documentation

If you ever get stuck with SELinux, refer to the documentation (at `http://selinuxproject.org/page/Main_Page`), which provides a few words of advice. There are very common reasons why SELinux might deny access to something on a system. First, it might be because someone or something has tried to get access to the system. Second, there might be a typo (or equally a bug) in a policy or simply an incorrectly named file somewhere. Finally, the docs suggest that a process might also be running under the wrong security context and hitting rules that aren't intended for it.

Clearly the log files are key to making sense of any issue. On some builds you can find the pertinent information in the file `/var/log/audit/audit.log`, which is provided courtesy of the `auditd` daemon. Needless to say, that path will be relatively similar if you can't find the file on your distribution. If for some reason `auditd` isn't available to perform the logging, you can look for information inside `/var/log/messages`.

■ **Tip** If your SELinux logs are buried among the noisy system detritus in logs, you can usually grep for the mention of AVC in order to highlight the SELinux entries. To look deeper, try "grepping" for SELinux in `/var/log/messages` with a string such as `"SELinux is preventing"`.

Checking multiple identities: If you ever wanted to determine how SELinux perceives you as a user (or any user that you have used the `su` command to become for that matter), use this command:

```
# id -Z
user_u:system_r:unconfined_t:s0
```

If you want to add users or groups to SELinux, simply use the useradd and groupadd commands as usual. If for one reason or another, a SELinux identity doesn't exist, SELinux will simply assign the user_u identity, which will be limited to the most basic tasks.

Graphical User Interface Tools

If you're troubleshooting (and using a Windows Manager), you can launch a GUI by installing the following packages:

```
# yum install setroubleshoot setools
```

Without running a Window Manager, that web page talks about other tools. You can also use sealert on some builds apparently:

```
# sealert -a /var/log/audit/audit.log > /path/to/chris_eyestrain.log
```

Use the previous example to scrutinize the log file, /path/to/chris_eyestrain.log, which will shed more light on any issues you encounter.

Another GUI tool that might come in handy is called apol; it offers the ability to study all the main facets relating to SELinux. It can also allow you to analyze actions such as domain transitions, where a process executes and needs to change the process's domain to a new type. Clever by design, apol can reuse any of your saved queries and hunt down information leaks and unwanted transitions when a process wants to access another domain.

■ **Note** There's a lot more to apol and I encourage you to read up on it if you want to deploy SELinux. For an easy read, go to https://access.redhat.com/documentation/en-US/Red_Hat_Enterprise_Linux/4/html/ SELinux_Guide/rhlcommon-section-0104.html.

---

audit2allow

As a last resort, you can also use the audit2allow command to create a custom policy module. This tool will allow you to pull information from SELinux log files pertaining to denials that have been triggered. You can start by searching all the audit logs (with -a) and produce something vaguely human-readable with the -w flag.

```
# audit2allow -w -a
```

The following commands generally need to be run as the root user.

```
# audit2allow -w -a
```

You can also run this command without the -w and see a more succinct error message showing what was violated. Once you have displayed the rule in question, you can run this command:

```
# audit2allow -a -M new_custom_module
```

The -M writes to a .te file (type enforcement file) with the name new_custom_module in this case. audit2allow will kindly compile your .te file into a .pp policy package file. You can then add the freshly built module as follows:

```
# /usr/sbin/semodule -i new_custom_module.pp Use this mode of access with caution.
```

To cope with the scenario where many restrictions from lots of processes are alerting you, but you only want to allow a single process, you can create a policy quite easily (but be careful) by grepping out the process in question as follows:

```
# grep process_name /var/log/audit/audit.log | audit2allow -M custom_module
```

Grub Bootloader

Should you ever get truly stuck with so-called "silent denials," this page is a good starting point: http:// docs.fedoraproject.org/en-US/Fedora/13/html/Security-Enhanced_Linux/sect-Security-Enhanced_ Linux-Fixing_Problems-Possible_Causes_of_Silent_Denials.html.

You also have the option to change your bootloader's parameters (via a console on a virtual machine or physically at a server for example), you can add the line enforcing=0 to your start-up config and you will switch SELinux to permissive mode so that your machine will boot (even if that means there will be a mountain of errors logged).

In Grub, you should add SELinux to the kernel line. Just do something like this in the Grub editor:

```
-> kernel /boot/vmlinuz-3.7.10-selinux-20151111 ro root=/dev/sde1 enforcing=0
```

Disabling SELinux

To completely disable SELinux, you have a couple of options. You can always add selinux=0 to the kernel boot parameters. This will completely disable SELinux and might be needed if your operating system doesn't have the /etc/selinux/config file present. This disables file labeling and process labeling. However, flavors such as Fedora and RHEL simply need SELINUX=disabled adjusted in /etc/selinux/config. Without that config file, you will most likely need to reboot to disable SELinux.

You can also jump between modes on running systems like this (shown here with a 0 for off; changing that to a 1 turns SELinux rules back on):

```
echo "0" > /selinux/enforce
```

That setting will remain until you issue the reverse of this command or reboot the system.

■ **Tip**   If it's possible, you might consider keeping a non-SELinux kernel available to boot with (especially if you're adding SELinux to an existing server) in case it causes headaches.

AVCstat

In case you need more help, there's a tool called avcstat that reports the status of AVC (Access Vector Cache), which runs the policy loaded by SELinux.

You can monitor the usage of SELinux as follows:

```
# /usr/sbin/avcstat
```

The output of such a command might be:

```
lookups hits misses allocs reclaims frees
1920881754 1920456664 425090 429063 424464 428552
```

The AVC cache will help you decide whether your system is performing as it should. If the number of lookups is double the number of the system hits, then your machine is under-performing.

There's a nice built-in addition that you can run in a console while troubleshooting; it adds a five-second refresh:

```
# /usr/sbin/avcstat 5
```

Sesearch

Another tool is called sesearch, and it lets you hunt down the source type, destination type, or class and look through an entire policy to get a result. The command for using sesearch might look something like this, for example:

```
# /usr/bin/sesearch -a -t httpd_sys_content_t /etc/selinux/targeted/polcy/policy.18
```

The -a asks for a display of all the rules that match the type httpd_sys_content_t in the specified policy (policy.18 in this case).

Looking at the /etc/selinux/targeted directory further, you can see that the targeted/contexts directory holds the following files and directories:

```
customizable_types default_type initrc_context securetty_types virtual_domain_context
dbus_contexts failsafe_context netfilter_contexts userhelper_context virtual_image_context
default_contexts files/ removable_context users/
```

Consider some of the types and contexts that SELinux uses. When you look inside the customizable_types file, you can see a list of types:

```
httpd_cvs_script_rw_t
httpd_squid_content_t
httpd_squid_htaccess_t
httpd_squid_script_exec_t
httpd_squid_script_ra_t
httpd_squid_script_ro_t
httpd_squid_script_rw_t
httpd_sys_content_t
httpd_sys_htaccess_t
httpd_sys_script_exec_t
httpd_sys_script_ra_t
```

```
httpd_sys_script_ro_t
httpd_sys_script_rw_t
httpd_unconfined_script_exec_t
mount_loopback_t
public_content_rw_t
public_content_t
samba_share_t
swapfile_t
xen_image_t
```

The file called `default_type` tells you that anything without a label will be automatically labeled as `system_r:unconfined_t`.

Summary

This chapter explored a number of the areas that SELinux encompasses. The chapter started with the basics, to installing SELinux on an existing server, to how contexts work, and how to make any changes persistent all the way through to troubleshooting issues. There is still much to learn however.

Some sysadmins are so convinced of SELinux's reliability and efficacy that remarkably they offer a demonstration machine that you can log in to as the superuser! That's correct, full root access. You can try this here: `http://www.coker.com.au/selinux/play.html`.

It's certainly an eye-opener. The sky is the limit with how far you want to get involved with SELinux, but hopefully you now feel confident enough to at least get started. And if you get stuck, there's always the NSA mailing list and a searchable archive that can be found at `http://marc.theaimsgroup.com/?l=selinux`.

One final avenue for help is to use some of the auto-generation tools available for policies, such as these: `https://fedoraproject.org/wiki/SELinux/PolicyGenTools`. At the very least, you can compare your rules with those produced for you in order to find any misconfigurations. In the interest of being able to run super-secure systems, the initial learning curve is well worth tackling.

CHAPTER 11

■ ■ ■

Nattier Networks

If you're a sysadmin who faces networking challenges on a daily basis, there's a reasonable chance that you have picked up the essentials as well as a few extras along the way. Don't get me wrong, it's absolutely fine to only learn what you need to if the majority of your day is spent software patching and not concerned with networking.

In this chapter, I intend to avoid the full "Networking 101" explanation of how, what, why, and where but instead extol the virtue of the ip command to help you pick up some more of the basics. I'll begin with a review of the older networking tool that many sysadmins used first, ifconfig.

Old School: Using ifconfig

The first tool I was exposed to for checking which IP address was in use on a server (or a Linux machine of any variety), was ifconfig. To find out which IP address is bound on each interface, I used:

```
# ifconfig -a
```

Make no mistake, the ifconfig utility comes a close second in ruling the networking landscape, but ultimately falls short behind the superior ip. Listing 11-1 provides a list of its supported hardware types for example.

Listing 11-1. The ifconfig Utility Is No Slouch Itself and Supports All Sorts of Network Types

```
loop (Local Loopback) slip (Serial Line IP) cslip (VJ Serial Line IP)
slip6 (6-bit Serial Line IP) cslip6 (VJ 6-bit Serial Line IP) adaptive
(Adaptive Serial Line IP)
strip (Metricom Starmode IP) ash (Ash) ether (Ethernet)
tr (16/4 Mbps Token Ring) tr (16/4 Mbps Token Ring (New)) ax25 (AMPR AX.25)
netrom (AMPR NET/ROM) rose (AMPR ROSE) tunnel (IPIP Tunnel)
ppp (Point-to-Point Protocol) hdlc ((Cisco)-HDLC) lapb (LAPB)
arcnet (ARCnet) dlci (Frame Relay DLCI) frad (Frame Relay Access Device)
sit (IPv6-in-IPv4) fddi (Fiber Distributed Data Interface) hippi (HIPPI)
irda (IrLAP) ec (Econet) x25 (generic X.25)
infiniband (InfiniBand)
```

The ifconfig utility's manual offers some useful details, including that it gleans its information from these files presented to the system by the pseudo-filesystem /proc:

```
/proc/net/socket
/proc/net/dev
/proc/net/if_inet6
```

Sadly, however, without having to squint in the slightest, at the top of the ifconfig utility's manual the "NOTE" section laments:

```
"This program is obsolete!  For replacement check ip addr and ip link. For statistics use ip
-s link".
```

Indeed, the ip command is both beautifully short to type and brimming with functionality.

New School: Using ip

Consider the ip equivalent of the ifconfig -a command:

```
# ip -s link
```

Listing 11-2 shows the output from that short command.

Listing 11-2. Useful Statistics from the ip -s link Command

```
1: lo: <LOOPBACK,UP,LOWER_UP> mtu 65536 qdisc noqueue state UNKNOWN
    link/loopback 00:00:00:00:00:00 brd 00:00:00:00:00:00
    RX: bytes  packets  errors  dropped overrun mcast
    3504956    55996    0       0       0       0
    TX: bytes  packets  errors  dropped carrier collsns
    3504956    55996    0       0       0       0
2: eth0: <BROADCAST,MULTICAST,UP,LOWER_UP> mtu 1500 qdisc mq state UP qlen 1000
    link/ether 00:30:14:2d:1a:ec brd ff:ff:ff:ff:ff:ff
    RX: bytes  packets  errors  dropped overrun mcast
    770413813  44919870 0       0       0       0
    TX: bytes  packets  errors  dropped carrier collsns
    1762383491 5460232  0       0       0       0
```

Incidentally, you can just look at the network interface eth0 with this command, as opposed to viewing all the interfaces using the previous one:

```
# ip -s link show dev eth0
```

The first element that my eye is drawn to in Listing 11-2 is the individual RX (received) and TX (transmitted) errors. This is thanks to the fact that I had all sorts of fun and games with Network Interface Card (NIC) drivers misbehaving in the past.

Generally speaking, however, when you push an inordinate amount of traffic through any NIC you can expect a few errors. A novice may just think I'm talking about the "errors" column, but actually I'm including "errors dropped overrun" for RX and "errors dropped carrier collsns" for TX. The latter TX statistics are for collisions (which is when two network interfaces on the same network try to send data at the same time and packets are dropped as a result).

Probably most important of all is the word UP on the top line in Listing 11-2 shown under the eth0 interface. This means the interface is enabled.

Next, I'll look at some of the many options that the ip command offers.

Old versus New

As I've mentioned, I was used to adding/checking/changing IP addresses with the ifconfig command previously. It might be useful to check against the equivalent command syntax with the newer utility and the ifconfig command. Here is ifconfig's syntax for adding an IP address:

```
# ifconfig eth0 10.10.2.125 netmask 255.255.255.0 broadcast 10.10.2.255
```

This command applies all three IP address settings to the eth0 interface, each of which can be added or changed individually. You simply remove the other one or two settings to ignore applying them.

The ip command's counterpart looks like this:

```
# ip addr add 10.10.2.125/24 dev eth0
```

This adds the IP address to the interface (and overwrites the settings associated with an existing IP address on that interface if they change). The shorthand version of ip addr is as follows:

```
# ip a
```

This next command provides part of the output of ifconfig -a shown earlier. It can get a little confusing at points, but it's not uncommon to type this shorthand for speed too (with the double a):

```
# ip a a 10.10.2.125/24 dev eth0
```

I've been a little remiss by only implicitly declaring the broadcast address of the IP address and subnet. I was explicit with the ifconfig example, so for the purposes of completion, here it is (added separately, explicitly):

```
# ip a a broadcast 10.10.2.255 dev eth0
```

There is obviously a need for some caution here with the command below, especially if you are logged in remotely over SSH and removing an IP address is as simple as accidentally deleting the IP address that you are connected to.

```
# ip a del 10.10.2.125/24 dev eth0
```

Remember I mentioned the ifconfig utility's "up" and whether that interface was enabled? It's just as easy to alter with the ip command.

```
# ip link set eth0 up
```

And, conversely, down works if you swap it in place of up in order to enable and disable an interface.

Jumbo Frames

Occasionally you need to adjust a network's Maximum Transmission Unit (MTU). Of course, you can break TCP horribly too, but if you're running fast networks (yes, I'm including gigabit networks) then moving the MTU from the bog-standard 1500 bytes to 9000 bytes can be achieved like this to potentially decrease CPU cycles on the networking kit and improve performance:

```
# ip link set mtu 9000 dev eth0
```

You use this command to check that your new MTU value of 9000 bytes has been applied:

```
# ip l sh eth0
```

Here is the output:

```
2: eth0: <BROADCAST,MULTICAST,UP,LOWER_UP> mtu 9000 qdisc mq state UP qlen 1000
    link/ether 00:42:13:4d:2a:ac brd ff:ff:ff:ff:ff:ff
```

The command ip l sh eth0 is the shorthand of the following command:

```
# ip link show eth0
```

IPv4 and IPv6

If you're operating in one of those lucky countries to have a decent adoption of IPv6 (I'm pointing the finger here squarely at the UK where, as I'm ashamed to say that we're significantly behind according to Google: https://www.google.com/intl/en/ipv6/statistics.html#tab=per-country-ipv6-adoption), then you can ignore IPv4 and focus on IPv6 interfaces (and vice versa with a "4") as follows:

```
# ip -6 a
```

There's also a very useful list command that I'll leave you to guess the shorthand for. To check which interfaces are up, you use:

```
# ip link ls up
```

The route Command

Along the same vein as the now deprecated ifconfig utility, the route command is a little long-in-the-tooth too. It almost brings a tear to my eye to read this under the "NOTE" section of the route command's manual:

"This program is obsolete. For replacement check ip route."

Fear not, though, as you can do all sorts of things with the ip command. Routing is unquestionably an integral part of the ip command's raison d'etre.

Embracing all things that mean less typing, you can use the perfectly short ip r command in order to check the local routing table of a machine by running the following command:

```
# ip r
```

Here is the output:

```
10.10.0.0/22 dev eth0  proto kernel  scope link  src 10.10.2.34
default via 10.10.0.1 dev eth0
```

The first line tells you that there's a routing entry for the 10.10.0.0 network on eth0 for the IP address 10.10.2.34. The second line tells you that if you need to contact any other network, you should forward your requests to the helpful 10.10.0.1 IP address because that's the helpful "default gateway" or "default route".

Consider the route command with DNS lookups switched off to lessen the burden on DNS servers and improve your screen's output:

```
# route -n
```

In Listing 11-3, you can see the results from running route -n on a very small routing table in this case. Incidentally, at the time of writing there are apparently around "562117" routes held in the global BGP routing table. If you're interested, there's some excellent information here: http://bgp.potaroo.net.

Listing 11-3. The Local Routing Table Is Displayed Old School, the Way It Was Meant to Be, Using route -n

```
Kernel IP routing table
Destination    Gateway      Genmask      lags  Metric Ref  Use  Iface
10.10.0.0      0.0.0.0      255.255.252.0  U      0     0    0    eth0
0.0.0.0        10.10.0.1    0.0.0.0        UG     0     0    0    eth0
```

It's worth noting that Listing 11-3 isn't volunteering the IP address that corresponds to the 10.10.0.0 network destination, unlike the output from the ip r command.

Now that you can view the routing table, let's take a look at manipulating it.

Static Routes

If you don't want to communicate with a network (or IP address) via the default route, you can easily add what's known as a "static route".

■ **Note**   A quick reminder for those new to this. The "default gateway" is the "default route" of which I speak. It catches all communication requests that don't have specific routing entries, such as the one that you're about to add by using a default route.

The static route syntax looks like this:

```
# ip route add 154.30.109.0/24 via 10.10.0.4 dev eth0
```

In simple terms, this states that any traffic for the 254 hosts on the 154.30.109.0 network should be sent via the gateway 10.10.0.4 and use the eth0 interface.

A reminder of the way it was written with the mighty route command is as follows. You can see that it's far from dissimilar to the ifconfig syntax you saw earlier:

```
# route add -net 154.30.109.0/24 netmask 255.255.255.0 gw 10.10.0.4
```

Hopefully, it's self-explanatory. The gw appendage obviously stands for "gateway". The only thing to note is the potential pitfall of the -net switch. The old route command was more concerned with being told about if you just wanted to redirect traffic to a new gateway for a single IP address or a whole network. The new kid on the block, however, figures that out with CIDR (Classless Inter-Domain Routing) formatting. That's the /24 in this case: 154.30.109.0/24.

The way that the old route command preferred to reference individual hosts was as follows with the -host adjustment (I've arbitrarily added 222 as the single IP address):

```
# route add -host 154.30.109.222 gw 10.10.0.4
```

However, a large number of Unix-like versions/distributions don't mind this shortened version too:

```
# route add 154.30.109.222 gw 10.10.0.4
```

Deleting a route is frighteningly simple. It's as easy as this command:

```
# ip route del 154.30.109.0/24 dev eth0
```

In the past if you wanted to alter the default route (clearly you know by now that I also mean the "gateway"), you would run the route command below. You have to do this carefully (!) and ideally use out-of-band access or SSHed in from another machine on the same LAN so that you didn't mind losing the default route.

For deleting a default route, compare the old and the new:

```
# route del default gw
# ip route del default
```

Adding a new default route is shown next; old and then new commands compared again:

```
# route add default gw 10.10.0.1 eth0
# ip route add default via 10.10.0.1 eth0
```

Clearly it's useful to mix and match these commands when using older operating systems. For example, I can easily commit route del default gw to memory it seems, but I frequently forget the ip route del default command.

Address Resolution Protocol

Another of my favorite protocols is the Address Resolution Protocol (ARP). It's simple, it's fast, and it is absolutely necessary to keep your machine on the network. The robust ip command does not shy away from ARP either.

As in the previous section, I'll provide old and new commands for comparison. Again with the arp command, I immediately use the -n switch without a second thought to avoid DNS load and latency.

Listing 11-4 shows which of the local hosts on the local area network (or within the VLAN—Virtual LAN) have recently communicated with the machine and registered an ARP entry as a result.

Listing 11-4. The Two Example Gateways Have Both Communicated with the Machine and Have Been Registered in the ARP Cache

```
# arp -n

Address          HWtype          HWaddress    Flags Mask     Iface
10.10.0.1        ether    00:a0:a3:e2:01:eb             C     eth0
10.10.0.4        ether    00:10:73:5a:26:12             C     eth0
```

One caveat is that I've heard some people (probably incorrectly) refer to the ARP "table," but I suspect it should really be referred to as the ARP *cache*. In essence it's a cache of machine IDs, involved in recent communications, within which each entry expires periodically, after a set expiration time. If you want to increase your ARP expiration knowledge about timeouts then there's a nice answer here: http://stackoverflow.com/questions/15372011/configuring-arp-age-timeout. The long and short of it is that don't just make a change to your kernel settings without understanding what you're doing first.

The equivalent syntax from the ip command is as follows and provides the output in Listing 11-5.

Listing 11-5. The Newer Type of Output Is Shown Using the ip n sh Command

```
# ip n sh

10.10.0.1 dev eth0 lladdr 00:a0:a3:e2:01:eb STALE
10.10.0.4 dev eth0 lladdr 00:10:73:5a:26:12 DELAY
```

Above you saw the shorthand, which is a more convenient way of expressing the following:

```
# ip neighbor show
```

Note the reference to STALE and DELAY in the newer style of output. A STALE neighbor is one that hasn't been spoken to for a while. The kernel probably assumes it's not available. A neighbor entry exhibiting a DELAY means that the kernel is dutifully trying to check in with the host but hasn't received any response. The REACHABLE host is, ahem, reachable, as you might imagine.

To add an entry to your ARP cache, you can simply use this command by associating the correct, hopefully unique (locally at least), MAC (Media Access Control) address with the IP address in question as follows:

```
# ip neigh add 10.10.3.2 lladdr 00:4d:20:15:b3:00 dev eth0
```

To delete an entry, use this:

```
# ip neigh del 10.10.3.2 dev eth0
```

Sometimes it is necessary to force an entry so it won't expire from the cache. You can do this with a simple appendage to the longer command. Apparently, the nud variable stands for "Neighbor Unreachability Detection".

The "permanent" switch has been covered and once added needs to be manually removed. The noarp option forces ARP to believe that this entry is kosher and it shouldn't attempt to check otherwise (it will just disappear as usual when its lifetime expires). The adjustable reachable option is as I've mentioned and the stale option means that ARP should treat an entry suspiciously, even though that ARP has recognized it as a valid entry.

An example nud addition to the previous command might be like this:

```
# ip neigh add 10.10.3.2 lladdr 00:4d:20:15:b3:00 dev eth0 nud perm
```

Now that you're fully versant in all things networking, I'm sure that you get the idea.

One final thing to look at with ARP is being able to flush your entire ARP cache. It's easy to do. There is some overhead, but if you're feeling brave you can empty the cache. You can flush the whole ARP cache using this ip command:

```
# ip -s -s neigh flush all
```

In case you think you're seeing double, the first -s adds greater levels of detail and stands for -statistics. The second points you at the "neighbor" table.

For comparison, in the olden days you might have cleared one IP address' entry as follows:

```
# arp -d 12.34.45.78
```

Banning Hosts

My favorite functionality available in Linux routing is being able to immediately ban a miscreant from getting access to my machine. (There are a few caveats of course; for one, you need the machine upstream to you, i.e., to your nearest router or gateway, to deflect the traffic so it gets nowhere near to your machine.) The following is still very useful in some circumstances such as minor Denial of Service (DoS) attacks.

The functionality I'm referring to has different names. The ip command's manual refers to adding a "blackhole". This is when traffic is not responded to but instead simply thrown into the "bit bucket," which is a bottomless pit where unwanted traffic is sent. Imagine it's like /dev/null on your filesystem. And, on that note, blackholing a route is called adding a "null route," because traffic is "nulled" or has nowhere to go. It's nipped in the bud and without wasting resources to respond to it with helpful errors in most cases.

An example of blocking such a nefarious route might look like this:

```
# ip route add blackhole 102.134.1.197/32
```

As you'd expect, you simply swap add with del to remove a route.

If you then run this command, you can check that it has been inserted into the local routing table. Its output is shown here:

```
# ip route show

default via 10.10.0.1 dev eth0 metric 100
blackhole 102.134.1.197
```

If you're interested, back in the day, you might have achieved similar results as follows:

```
# route add -host 102.134.1.197 reject
```

Summary

For some readers, this chapter may have just been a refresher but for those new to networking or to the iproute2 package, hopefully it's a concise enough reference guide for the future.

With one package or another, sometimes a quick check on syntax that you've had positive results from in the past is necessary. Sysadmins have all sorts of ways to remember fiddly formatting and I tend to have an ever-growing text file that I should really add to a "Git repository" because it's cumbersome. To the newbies, please take heed and use these commands carefully. You should ideally test them on a development machine before wildly breaking things and irritating your employer or users.

It is important to be able to quickly recall the simple commands. I am forever using the shorthand ip a command, for example, which saves lots of typing along with the ability to append an IP address to an interface without having to look it up. As a result, when looking up help files or man pages, the remaining syntax is absorbed much quicker and causes less eyestrain. It is worth using the flexible ip command frequently until the syntax sinks in. It will almost definitely assist you in a crisis.

■ ■ ■

## CHAPTER 12

Keeping Information Private with GPG

Many people have heard of Pretty Good Privacy (PGP) before. Even the non-technical among us might recognize the unusual name. It has been unquestionably key in furthering the public-at-large's use of encryption to protect their privacy for many years. Reportedly it is also the most widely used cryptographic tool globally.

PGP can be used for all sorts of things; when it comes to e-mail for example PGP can digitally sign e-mails or fully encrypt their contents. Anything that you want, within reason, can be encrypted with PGP. Licensing, patents, and re-branding have played their part with the classic PGP, however. Several years ago, partly due to the relatively public airings of concerns, a standard called "OpenPGP" arose. Today a number of Apple iOS and Google Android applications take advantage of OpenPGP, utilizing its best-of-breed pedigree and robust encryption, as well as certain e-mail clients. Even popular web browsers such as Mozilla Firefox use extensions such as "Enigform" to sign HTTP requests. It is therefore safe to say that OpenPGP will continue to advance into the Cloud and beyond due to its undoubted strengths.

This chapter takes a look at a GPL-licensed (General Public Licensed) version of PGP called "GNU Privacy Guard" (also known as "GnuPG" or "GPG"). I'll provide enough technical information so that can understand what's going on behind the scenes and then I'll translate that knowledge into a GUI-driven encryption solution for Google's Gmail.

GPG Is Open and Free

The GPL license effectively makes GPG free to use and fully open to endless community improvement through constructive input. It's the GNU way and to my mind this is the way that all software should be shared. Although it's all essentially part of the same family (in other words, it's OpenPGP-compliant), it's worth noting that certain PGP versions simply won't work with other OpenPGP systems. So beware and make sure you can decrypt a piece of sensitive data successfully before blindly destroying it, especially if it's set to traverse across across the Internet destined for a different-flavored system.

If I wanted to check on my Debian-based Ubuntu system when GPG was installed and whether it was part of the standard installation or or a package of its own (which means it might have been tampered with), I could do this with a quick one-liner:

```
# grep install /var/log/dpkg.log | grep gpg
```

Remove | grep gpg to get more information about other packages' installation dates if you like.

Running GPG

To see a list of all available options, run --dump-options in the terminal:

```
# gpg --dump-options
```

Listing 12-1 shows an abbreviated list of the output, which is too long to show in full here.

Listing 12-1. An Abbreviated List of a Small Number of the Sophisticated GPG's Feature List

```
--sign
--clearsign
--detach-sign
--encrypt
--encrypt-files
--symmetric
--store
--decrypt
--decrypt-files
--verify
--verify-files
--list-keys
--list-public-keys
--list-sigs
--check-sigs
--fingerprint
--list-secret-keys
--gen-key
--delete-keys
```

Some options include a reference to Request For Comments (RFCs) texts. You can see these options (as opposed to commands) by using this:

```
# gpg --dump-options | grep rfc
--rfc1991
--rfc2440
--rfc4880
--rfc2440-text
--no-rfc2440-text
```

The RFC that I'll look at is RFC 4880; when I run the following command for the first time I get the output shown in Figure 12-1.

```
# gpg --rfc4880
```

```
gpg: directory `/home/chris/.gnupg' created
gpg: new configuration file `/home/chris/.gnupg/gpg.conf' created
gpg: WARNING: options in `/home/chris/.gnupg/gpg.conf' are not yet active during this run
gpg: keyring `/home/chris/.gnupg/secring.gpg' created
gpg: keyring `/home/chris/.gnupg/pubring.gpg' created
gpg: Go ahead and type your message ...
```

Figure 12-1. The first time you run GPG, your home directory receives a few additions

As shown in Figure 12-1, choosing an RFC does more than one might expect. It reveals that the directory /home/chris is populated with the subdirectory .gnupg/, which then gets a config file and two binary keyring files. You're also asked to type a message to encrypt, which you can safely ignore for now.

■ **Note**   No one except you should have access to the private key (absolutely nobody). Whereas everyone should have access to your public key. The premise being that if someone wants to encrypt a message to you, they use your public key to wrap it up and only your private key can decrypt it. Simple really.

When I added the --rfc4880 flag to run GPG, I ensured that I activated its OpenPGP-compliant functionality. This makes compatibility more likely. In fact, I could also call this option with --openpgp. The digest, used to assist with restoring a corrupt file, becomes strictly RFC 4880 compliant as does the cipher (encryption algorithm) and packet options. Clearly, the other options relating RFCs will trigger other compliancy settings.

Config Files

Next, I'll take a closer look at files created in the home directory by GPG. The new keyring files, as you might expect, are empty until you populate them with keys. The gpg.conf config file is brimming with options and too long to expose here. I will however get GPG up and running with some basic features, which will hopefully fuel your enthusiasm enough to explore more advanced options.

If you run GPG without options, then GPG does some intelligent rooting around and tries to decide what you want it to do. For example, it will attempt to decrypt a message if presented with one that is encrypted, it might try to verify a signature that it sees, or a keyfile might have its key contents listed.

Try the --gen-key option and generate a new key pair to fill up your home directory's empty files. Figure 12-2 shows what happens when you run the following:

```
# gpg --gen-key
```

```
Mia .gnupg # gpg --gen-key
gpg (GnuPG) 1.4.18; Copyright (C) 2014 Free Software Foundation, Inc.
This is free software: you are free to change and redistribute it.
There is NO WARRANTY, to the extent permitted by law.

Please select what kind of key you want:
   (1) RSA and RSA (default)
   (2) DSA and Elgamal
   (3) DSA (sign only)
   (4) RSA (sign only)
Your selection?
```

Figure 12-2. You are asked the type of keys you want to generate by GPG

If you choose the default RSA keys with "(1) RSA and RSA (default)," you are then asked the following:

```
RSA keys may be between 1024 and 4096 bits long.
What keysize do you want? (2048)
```

Again, go for the default, which is relatively beefy encryption at 2,048 bits. Then enter an expiry date at 0, which means the keys will never expire. Next, you are asked to provide your name and e-mail; you can leave the comment empty if you wish. You are shown how you are presented to the outside world to make sure it's right and then you get the most important choice of all ... the passphrase.

I cannot emphasize enough how important it is to remember the passphrase (but don't write it down) and also to make it very lengthy and strong. I enjoy checking how inadequate my passwords are using this excellent site: https://howsecureismypassword.net.

When it comes to passphrases, you can't go wrong creating very long obfuscated sentences as opposed to short complex ones. You'll know what I mean after visiting the previously mentioned password-checking site: make it at least a million years!

Random Data

After entering your passphrase, you need to enter lots of random data in this next step. You are told the following:

```
We need to generate a lot of random bytes. It is a good idea to perform some other action
(type on the keyboard, move the mouse, utilize the disks) during the prime generation; this
gives the random number generator a better chance to gain enough entropy.
```

When finished, GPG reports what had completed the key creation process, as seen in Listing 12-2.

Listing 12-2. You're Now Ready to Start Using GPG for Encryption Having Created Your Keys

```
eygrflie7gfp927gh8fpgpg: /home/chris/.gnupg/trustdb.gpg: trustdb created
gpg: key 67491897 marked as ultimately trusted
public and secret key created and signed.

gpg: checking the trustdb
gpg: 3 marginal(s) needed, 1 complete(s) needed, PGP trust model
gpg: depth: 0  valid:   1  signed:   0  trust: 0-, 0q, 0n, 0m, 0f, 1u
pub   2048R/67491897 2014-11-22
      Key fingerprint = 59A8 C269 B197 C166 5715  1577 5EA4 EEAE 6749 1897
uid                  Chris Binnie <chris@binnie.tld>
sub   2048R/2FA73DD5 2014-11-22
```

Following that output from GPG, you now have lots of binary files in your hidden ~/.gnupg directory and only the .conf file is readable. A directory listing shows:

```
gpg.conf  pubring.gpg  pubring.gpg~  random_seed  secring.gpg  trustdb.gpg
```

The file name with the tilde is a backup file, in case you're wondering.

Next, you're going to generate an "armoured" key in ASCII. This is matched to the Unique Identifier ("uid") shown in Listing 12-2. You need a key for sharing with others and can achieve the output shown in Figure 12-3 (saved as the pubkey.asc file with this command):

```
# gpg --armour --export chris@binnie.tld > pubkey.asc
```

```
Mia .gnupg # cat pubkey.asc
-----BEGIN PGP PUBLIC KEY BLOCK-----
Version: GnuPG v1.4.12 (GNU/Linux)

mQINBFOm/wEBEACvlKrhJeBfNUjp6lkYCeHykRBPYzZNnMnoW8752B5bXtvSGXSX
6KzSGDnvJfR+hTgSHG85WTliR8ILuwQNBgl6YiMMsIkID9eVisJE0i8/QF3Ag8k7
+PiugDbRCMSr52pKmJhTXmV+gKdT7g6WkWOgDQvqvqoOg6vPmKm8zqAtmVdLWhm4
Hgx683KXD16OyfpbyXHAZPu5lEDrGvHpNGDbYUr88ojf7bmQi288kPWlrSaFtAun
9t752Bpcj9Y4KW2qkaISLfBMo/gF/k2O5HFkfReurngpEVSbDFqIeX375gS6mvuy
3soMF52YTWOxEeq78MFVXQxkjvr4btuWrhp/7ZFqplFLuLPhSUDAbHhrbjBE+2V5
gReg9trUXrl7aTy3eR6uWWsfT+fpwP8xiXXk8SkBJFmGb2YbRHaKajMCKe5ZA9Z/
okHtYLIrk7Lck3Obif9wjgT/hyv+llmftoZtXctsuYNzH/ODMKP6df4BblLMjrOs
jtD85qAy5kQX2M5tWVV6wqDUX4utPCE8hSaoyWVddiZrlw8bMd9hB+lyteplSuRl
023hpjETIvVflJoy1S+Tya8sIvt6v9krY8/q3faZOMhK+CD94IR5k65L/wARAQAB
tEBCYXJ0IElhcnRlbnMgKGZvciBlc2UgaW4gZmxhc2hwbHVhnaW4+tbm9uZnJlZSSkg
PGJhcnRtQGRlYmlhbi5vcmc+iQI3BBMBCAAhBQJTpv8BAhsDBQsJCAcDBRUKCQgL
UND2nHgwxolsyj9MXMDMDvTkZmfNPiYnpy12n+w3h5Fr/DP22rYjUE/sk5P1Z+/c
bIb+W+H7JjqJb+AKWtlMUOyFIonGCfWcrXCFYLdVIYrEF+aUvvqQzJdV/R/DnoBb
6vpYy85gvEqyshUdfyP3bOlDJDcz4tqmarChZO/uaGDaZ9BS7axYiNitjqseHsDk
2G5iWheNhjzh2S4O/WOc/lcqObTwapuls3LCypgbPOqFuLfM3F9loHJF5QVzD0QK
6KzSGDnvJfR+hTgSHG85WTliR8ILuwQNBgl6YiMMsIkID9eVisJE0i8/QF3Ag8k7
xpYTOZeYteMVK4QWpQjHdNUBwBD8+YqmcF5K+sLJxlrBPHatxZtB5SaNmXLY41Qk
6+E9cNkhd3KdqzXLrS4esUhvSl0kztTEjrKAfWcPb6SJlGRpTLl5WbAeEjbEMgwr
BBdofsZGPTbHwwGXFlQT49nDDGW99kYze4hfNZNVODF4fzEzbAr9XmzsMeZk8aOY
U/zQjzOofnnPI1XEOvYbTN8KA2EvOzt6xAJLJR/D8LsDuAXPocSIOssvL4Cii+Z8
ybDp8l8HGkLxHRp8p+fMJlXng6FN2PvnRO/nsOawT8DTF3kl6tdChnKCGhTibfFR
u7Xpdqa/Cm3d4GFE
=JKMY
-----END PGP PUBLIC KEY BLOCK-----
Mia .gnupg # █
```

Figure 12-3. *This file shows my public key, which I can safely leave lying around or e-mail to anyone that I wish without fear of my private key being discovered*

Encrypting a Message

You've seen how to tie certificates to your e-mail address (or "uid"), but what if someone changes the key (because they lost the old one) and you then need to remove them from your keyring (which is used when checking identities)? You can use the following command and the e-mail UID to remove a key:

```
# gpg --delete-key you-are-outta-here@binnie.tld
```

If you had a GPG installation yourself, you could easily encrypt a message and send it to me by doing the following:

```
# gpg --import chris-pubkey.asc
```

The imported key is added to your keyring. Next, compose a secret message, for example, "The magical Leo Messi," and save it as in.txt; this is the content/file you want to feed to GPG using the following command:

```
# gpg --encrypt -r chris@binnie.tld --armour < in.txt -o out.txt
```

The -r specifies which public key on your keyring you want to use. This is the command that you need to run to encrypt a message with my public key.

At this point, GPG creates an out.txt file with your encrypted message, as shown in Figure 12-4.

```
Mia .gnupg # cat out.txt
-----BEGIN PGP MESSAGE-----
Version: GnuPG v1

hQEMAO7kffZNidr6AQf/fWZIJqdQlozgWEmjlHs5+56a5DSM4DCDaloBulClF2Cq
HaAaLo6yQCOvr7igz+VQSD6vXXM3h14ZqFvxtPHVb/5tEaSEHo77n6eDSYreehQa
u4NB2AZvUdKE2tkjeKTbdzETJl5SoEzVQ2jiG9o9cbcVlqOwY5AEaBHkW1Sz7c9a
3sZ9QAL63VPDUQjErWLennUAm9yF+UFkHZiBON5MBYuf/y7Jy4xzdhZtRxJPrty6
af40D+3oMCMNt+50NqQoxAQdRvXkNg5/TtweVlARSrbSq+pLQTjnLzd5nPuzPsrw
XncK7gBqwreLfse/KbNfGngm6qxZQlVlcyUGOnqmpNJGAXrgOZWmC6t4QyRuOCuO
s7U4tPwHgWrw+vUzule32zFMQnIbhKlOCyTHzMp5NBXJwZNh/BMPH98UYEA3ifKx
2XVJr6/iZQ==
=aGDH
-----END PGP MESSAGE-----
Mia .gnupg # █
```

Figure 12-4. *The secret message is now encrypted and only my private key can translate it*

Decrypting a Message

In order to --decrypt the secret message, you need to type the following:

```
# gpg --decrypt out.txt
```

You'll be presented instantly with a passphrase prompt in order to unlock your private key. If that's successful, your secret message will appear, as shown in Listing 12-3.

Listing 12-3. Lo and Behold, the Secret Message, Now Decrypted

```
You need a passphrase to unlock the secret key for
user: "Chris Binnie <chris@binnie.tld>"
2048-bit RSA key, ID 2FA73DD5, created 2014-11-22 (main key ID 67491897)

gpg: gpg-agent is not available in this session
gpg: encrypted with 2048-bit RSA key, ID 2FA73DD5, created 2014-11-22
      "Chris Binnie <chris@binnie.tld>"
The magical Leo Messi
```

Caveats

It's important to have a cursory understanding of where the security strengths exist in GPG. By creating keys, you are using 2,048 bits (by default, and up to 4,906 bits with RSA is possible). That's really pretty strong, but if the passphrase for your keyring is weak *or* your user account on your laptop, desktop, or server is weak, then dictionary attacks can simply spend a little CPU time getting access to your private key. The passphrase is easily the weakest part of this process, so create one using a few words to lengthen it, obfuscated, as I've mentioned. Like this, but with numbers and symbols built in:

```
PassTheBallFortyYardsGerrard
```

You should also be fully aware that during a clear-text exchange over a network, your passphrase can easily be identified by network sniffing. So don't do it, ever!

Using Digital Signatures

You can also sign your messages using "digital signatures". This section explores some of the other functionality that GPG can offer. The following command assumes that you already have my public key on your keyring:

```
# gpg --import chris-pubkey.asc
```

If I wanted to send a readable message, which was guaranteed to come from me, I could do this simply by signing the message with GPG:

```
# gpg --sign in.txt
```

The result of this is saved in the in.txt.gpg file and GPG again asks for the password, as shown in this output:

```
You need a passphrase to unlock the secret key for
user: "Chris Binnie <chris@binnie.tld>"
2048-bit RSA key, ID 67491897, created 2014-11-22
```

Figure 12-5 shows that although my formerly secret message is no longer secret, there's an envelope (the digital signature) surrounding it that only GPG will understand, proving where it came from. Incidentally, if you wanted to output to a specific file name (possibly for use in scripts), you could add this: --output signed.sig, for example.

```
Mia .gnupg # cat in.txt.gpg
      E  "b  n.txtV$  The magical Leo Messi
       s  
        E :M x    s#fpG   d)z>     Q  "H  $r   REZ      S Q      #  -($
   h ;    i    r  g-  s  l    _u w ;= x$   c  , 7|Le  >       P  N ,     |U
                                                                    #
                                                              3      
                                                                         (
Mia .gnupg # ▌
```

Figure 12-5. *My secret message is no longer a secret even though it is wrapped up, compressed, and presented in binary mode*

As you might imagine, verifying, beyond doubt, that someone is who they say they are is a really big deal. Think about intelligence officers and the necessity of trusting that your orders are genuine while practising your tradecraft. The role of GPG is also imperative because, not only is your message sender verified, but so is the timestamp so you know that the data is new and current.

There is also a --clearsign signing option that might be useful for telling people that an e-mail definitely came from me or for adding a message on a web forum in order to quickly and simply confirm its authenticity and integrity. You can do this as follows, with textfile being the file that's holding your message:

```
# gpg --clearsign textfile
```

The result of this is a request for your passphrase in order to sign the document again. Once that input is received, a non-binary output file is generated as textfile.asc, as shown in Listing 12-4. There's no doubt who the message is from and when it was created, although for a short message it undeniably adds extra bulk, as you can see.

Listing 12-4. A Clearsigned Message Suitable for E-Mails and Posting

```
-----BEGIN PGP SIGNED MESSAGE-----
Hash: SHA1

All your base are belong to us.
-----BEGIN PGP SIGNATURE-----
Version: GnuPG v1.4.11 (GNU/Linux)

iQEcBAEBAgAGBQJUcX2+AAoJEF6k7q5nSRiXlGMIALlLSvS1lskMlkF4UvuXt6qN
yBW7mEBzVaG6HdHKHROLzVxSyMpafwuMqQrpnfqFQqPpK6Ii9HWG9+vY4Bc1QZO5
TeQSWkXk+uY1MBDlPW2+7KejxsnjSJFRqZmIiVGPB3x71aD7PWVpNRxOBGjkpOxs
ZOAiT7J7n2y9onhJ4BJQWeMaCScajBat8yugWn9t1Vc8ns48r6mz3uSdZaC1gkvC
iZ3j/XummMfWLiO8Rt8vMcqHTmMVkdABOqA7vSeEquuHOlGdmRlyyiJMfNVtOvHZ
uxYwLTUODOuduxtEpay/EEx/ZKD1X7CYSO44ouHE7hxBoRd9cW4nVaYatASNDYQ=
=WrDq
-----END PGP SIGNATURE-----
```

The third signing method is called "detached signatures". As previously mentioned, signed documents are a little cumbersome and limited in their immediate usefulness. Even with clearsigning, the end user must tinker with the signed document in order to read it. The other way of verifying the sender and the time is with a separate text file, saved separately from the message file, by using the `--detach-sig` option, as so:

```
# gpg --output ouputfile.sig --detach-sig inputfile
```

For this example, both the original message and the signed signature file are required to read and verify the message. You do this with the following command, referencing both files:

```
# gpg --verify textfile.sig textfile
```

Setting Up GPG in Google Chrome

Consider the scenario where you want to encrypt e-mails sent by your webmail provider. Let's take the very popular Gmail as an example and extend the GPG knowledge you have just picked up.

I'm going to use Google Chrome on my laptop to set up a clever lightweight extension called "Mymail-Crypt for Gmail" to make Google's Gmail work a little harder for me. Mymail-Crypt for Gmail supports OpenPGP and uses the `OpenPGP.js` library. You can download the extension here: `http://bit.ly/1FeSqmY`.

After adding the extension to the Chrome browser, click the Customize menu in the top-right side of the browser window and select More Tools ➤ Extensions. On the resulting Extensions page, locate Mymail-Crypt for Gmail (shown in Figure 12-6) and click Options to open the Mymail-Crypt for Gmail options page.

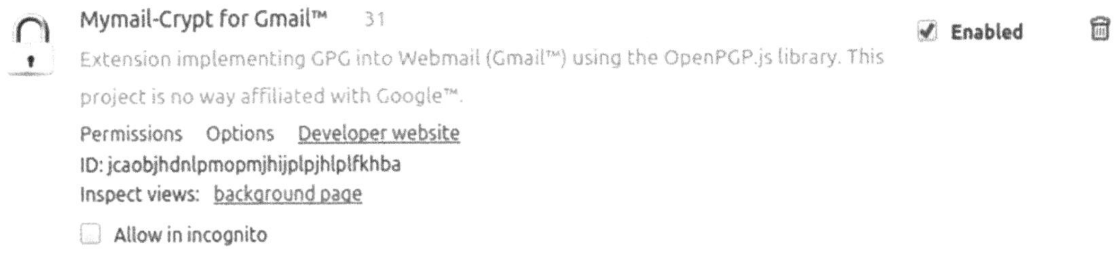

Figure 12-6. *Click Options to set up Mymail-Crypt for Gmail in Chrome*

Figure 12-7 shows the available options at the top of this page.

Figure 12-7. *How to configure Mymail-Crypt for Gmail*

Next, provide your private key. Click "my keys" and insert the private key from your pubkey.asc file. Incidentally, there's also an option for the extension to generate the keys for you, if you're so inclined. It's shown in Figure 12-8 and provides the same options that the command line presented previously.

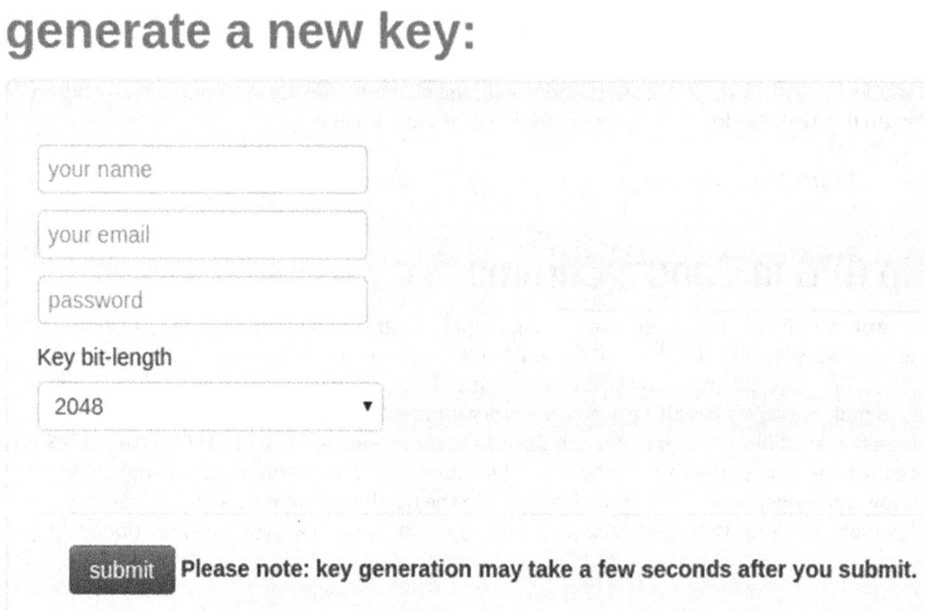

generate a new key:

| your name |
| your email |
| password |

Key bit-length

| 2048 ▼ |

submit   **Please note: key generation may take a few seconds after you submit.**

Figure 12-8. *Mymail-Crypt for Gmail will even generate a new key for you, up to 2,048 bits*

The only other section to be concerned with for getting started is adding your friend's keys. Mymail-Crypt for Gmail makes it very simple. Figure 12-9 shows how to add your entire social circle to your heart's content.

my friends' public keys:

| name | email | key id |

insert public key:

Figure 12-9. *How to add other people's public keys*

■ **Note**   Mymail-Crypt for Gmail makes a point of telling you *not* to use this extension on a shared computer, as keys are no longer safe. It suggests that multi-user access to the extension might be added as a feature in the future. It also states that "This extension supports a limited subset of the possible OpenPGP implementations. RSA/AES/SHA1/CAST128 are supported." It goes without saying (but I'll say it anyway) that you should make sure you're importing compatible keys to avoid headaches.

To verify your setup, you need to refresh your Gmail page with an F5 key tap or similar. Automagically, a number of options appear on your "Compose" e-mail boxes. (If that is not the case, try refreshing or even restarting Chrome.) Note also that your key should match your Gmail e-mail address and not an e-mail alias. You should see something similar to what is shown Figure 12-10 at the bottom right of your "Compose" dialog box (it looks a bit broken because of my screen size).

Figure 12-10. *You can now sign and fully encrypt messages with absolute ease*

At this point, you can see the simplicity of using a relatively complex process, and painlessly, for day-to-day use.

Summary

This chapter attempted to make sure that you have a firm grasp of the fundamentals before showing you the easy GUI-driven stuff. The importance of Internet privacy is perennially debated and something that the next generation of Internet users should be made fully aware of.

It is up to each user which level of encryption they deploy and where they use it. With GPG, you can now make those choices yourself.

CHAPTER 13

■ ■ ■

Get Permission from Your Peers with Sudo

I'm certain that most sysadmins have encountered a scenario in the past where it's become important to give a user access to an otherwise privileged resources on a server without giving them superuser access. And if you're an Ubuntu user, you will already be relatively used to the process of elevating your privileges to that of a superuser, all without directly typing su -.

The tool of choice in Ubuntu is sudo, which allows you to log in as a normal user. Then, by using sudo -i, you semi-permanently become the superuser, "root". It's worth saying that all the other distributions support sudo, but Ubuntu enforces its use for privileged elevation. The -i in this case apparently simulates an initial login and fires up the user's environment with a minimum number of variables, all in the same way as the hyphen in su -. Without that hyphen, su ignores some variables and doesn't change to the "root" user's home directory, which means that you can elevate your privileges in the directory in which you were previously working and carry on as before typing as a different user.

This chapter takes a more detailed look at sudo and hopefully you can then decide which aspects suit your needs.

Basics

I'm using Ubuntu as my operating system on a desktop, which employs sudo by default.

On Ubuntu, once you've elevated your privileges to the superuser, using any permutation of the sudo command, you have 15 minutes to run your commands before your user status is queried again. You're then prompted to re-enter your password following the expiration of its validity.

If you're running a simple command, then using something like this will work (and you will be prompted for a password after entering such, if you haven't recently):

```
# sudo less /etc/shadow
```

If you don't want to be pestered by environment issues and avoid prepending sudo to the front of each command, you can use this, which acts a bit like a normal "root" user login as we discussed a moment ago:

```
# sudo -i
```

Alternatively, a very similar command is using -s. This spawns a shell if one is specified; otherwise, a standard interactive shell is made available to you.

```
# sudo -s
```

If you fancy repeating a previous command, then it's nice and easy and can be achieved with:

```
# sudo !!
```

A useful addition to your command line toolkit is quickly revoking sudo access with the following, after you've finished with it, before letting a colleague type at your terminal (so if something goes wrong then your colleague's user is logged as using sudo to elevate privileges):

```
# sudo -k
```

You can also use sudo to run commands as a specific user (assuming that you're allowed to run commands as that user in the sudo rules of course) like this:

```
# sudo -u chrisbinnie "/usr/sbin/encrypt-a-secret"
```

The Main Config

Before taking a more detailed look at sudo's config, I'll begin with an example of how it expects its rules to look. Namely, the main config file called /etc/sudoers.

Thankfully, you can add aliases to your config file, which makes using sudo more pleasant. These aliases can look like this for three users under the BOFH and DEVS groups, for example:

```
User_Alias BOFH = chris,operator,hell
User_Alias DEVS = really,nice,people
```

In addition, you can also alias commands and group commands, which makes for a lot less typing and cutting and pasting, as so:

```
Cmnd_Alias SYSSTUFF       = /sbin/reboot, /sbin/poweroff, /usr/bin/kill, /sbin/shutdown
Cmnd_Alias TROUBLESHOOT   = /usr/bin/ngrep, /usr/sbin/ockhams-razor
```

You can also frequently refer to a host or group of hosts within your sudo rules. For example, with CRIX and BINNIX having unique IP addresses and subnets:

```
Host_Alias CRIX   = 10.10.10.10/24
Host_Alias BINNIX = 192.168.0.1/24
```

You can now see these rules taking form, using some of the simple examples above. See Listing 13-1.

Listing 13-1. These Simple Rules Are Beginning to Take On a Sensible Short-Handed Form

```
# Actual rules not definitions
root,BOFH ALL   = (ALL) NOPASSWD: ALL # Root and BOFH users can do anything with no passwd
DEVS      CRIX = (ALL) NOPASSWD: TROUBLESHOOT # DEVS can test on CRIX box with no passwd

# Any user can chuck a CD in the drive (and remove it)
ALL          ALL    = NOPASSWD: /sbin/mount /cdrom,/sbin/umount /cdrom
```

Using GUIs

Tools that provide sudo functionality for desktops and GUIs, rather than servers, include kdesudo on Kubuntu for the KDE desktop environment or gksudo, which is powered by GTK+ (the GIMP toolkit), on the Gnome desktop environment.

From a GUI perspective, Ubuntu also helpfully offers a "launcher" shortcut on Gnome. Create a launcher on your desktop with the following code as an example:

```
# gksudo "gnome-open %u"
```

The results are visible if you drag a file over to the launcher. Not only will the correct application open the file as if you had double-clicked it in the Nautilus file manager but it will also be opened as the "root" user. Think along the lines of gedit opening /etc/hosts. If you haven't already become the "root" user, then the file would open as read-only, making it impossible to edit, and cause a deep sigh when the realization falls upon you.

Using Terminals

Note that the centralized config file for a system, /etc/sudoers, is even read-only for the "root" user. Obviously, the "root" user still needs to be able to read it for clarity on the sudo rules being used. Listing 13-2 provides some empirical evidence of the permissions.

Listing 13-2. The /etc/sudoers File Is Even Locked Away from Being Edited by Root

```
# ls -hal /etc/sudoers
-r--r-----. 1 root root 4.0K Nov 11 11:11 /etc/sudoers

# stat -c "%a %n" /etc/sudoers
440 /etc/sudoers
```

That file is locked down so tightly because it should encourage sysadmins to use the approved editor rather than editing it directly. As an aside, if you've ever inserted a "crontab" entry for a specific user then you'll know what I mean. For example, you would edit your cron jobs using the "crontab" editor like so:

```
# crontab -e
```

That's not to say that vi, vim, pico, or nano won't edit this file for you, but as legend (and, ahem, the manual) has it, the odd 440 permissions are to get you to use the visudo editor. The theory being for example that, if a rogue special character (have you ever introduced an otherwise invisible character to a file unwittingly?) gets added inadvertently to the file /etc/sudoers, then there's a reasonable chance that no one will be able to get "root" access to the machine at all!

A little like the crontab -e editor, the clever "visudo" performs a syntax check at saving time to prevent you from breaking a production system with a single, superfluous ^M character.

For other config files relating to sudo there's a utility called sudoedit (which appears to actually just be the same as running sudo -e). Among other things, they can back up your config files temporarily before committing them to disk. Experiment with them as you see fit.

Editing Config

Incidentally when you try to engage sudo, you might be confronted with a welcome message similar to the one shown in Listing 13-3.

Listing 13-3. The Well-Known sudo Welcome Message

```
I trust you have received the usual lecture from the local system administrator. It usually
boils down to these three things:

    #1) Respect the privacy of others.
    #2) Think before you type.
    #3) With great power comes great responsibility.
```

Incidentally, anybody in the admin group by default will be able to elevate privileges by using sudo. The "wheel" group is popular on some distributions too. The entry looks like this in the config file (note the percentage sign):

```
# Members of the admin group are allowed to gain root privileges via sudo
%admin ALL=(ALL) ALL
```

Imagine that you need to add access for other users so that they can affect varying applications or config files on your precious system. From Debian Squeeze onward (and as a result this most likely applies to Ubuntu), you begin by adding the user to the correct system group, as follows:

```
# adduser chrisbinnie sudo
```

Here, my username chrisbinnie becomes a member of the correct group (sudo in this case). Of course, you may need to su - or prepend sudo to that command to gain the correct level of permissions to execute adduser.

Once you're added to the group sudo, you should log out and then back in again to ensure that you have the newly created sudo rights. A word of warning: the older versions of Ubuntu (pre-Long Term Support release, Precise—12.04) used to call the group admin and not sudo.

The first time that you look up your /etc/sudoers file, you can just launch:

```
# visudo
```

If there's any change to the default location of /etc/sudoers, then point visudo elsewhere:

```
# visudo -f /etc/sudoers
```

If you're not a vi fanatic, you can use other editors. For the vim editor, you run the following:

```
# export VISUAL=vim; visudo
```

And, to bring more color to your text editing life, try running this command for nano:

```
# export VISUAL=nano; visudo
```

There's also a way of adding a Defaults setting to the main config file, a little like this:

```
Defaults editor = /bin/nano
```

Incidentally, if you do mess up the main config file by using an editor other than visudo, then there's a well-known way of changing a forgotten root password in single-user mode should you need access to a system. The slick sudo accounts for this with an altered sulogin file when it's triggered by init, so you can rest a little easier at least. Utilize your favorite online searching device for more information.

Bugs and Threats

For those of you not updating the software on your servers frequently with security patches (you know who you are), here's a quick word of advice. For mission-critical servers, there was previously a very good reason why you would not want to use sudo. sudo looks for full paths for its commands. Users can potentially alter their paths to one of their allowed commands and elevate their user to having root privileges. An option was added to mitigate this when running sudo, namely --with-secure-path. Reading this bug entry means that your mileage might indeed vary however:

```
https://bugs.launchpad.net/ubuntu/+source/sudo/+bug/50797
```

A cursory online search suggests that this might help. It appears that enforcing sudo -i to ensure that $PATH is recognized or adding a Bash alias as follows might be the best way around the issue:

```
alias sudo="sudo env PATH=$PATH"
```

Adding the -i option emulates a shell login and tries to get environment variables and PATH to maintain some sanity. If this is a concern because you're stuck using an old version of sudo then you should definitely research this issue thoroughly.

The moral of this vignette is a simple one. All software has bugs, but not all open up your "root" account in quite the same way as sudo does:

```
http://www.sudo.ws/sudo/security.html
```

Most of the lines in your default main config are commented out. Apparently, the syntax takes a very specific format that was designed to help should your config file grow lengthy. The format is known as EBNF (Extended Backus-Naur Form). Once it is filled with user-defined configuration information, lines near the start can reference lines near the end of the file. In other words, your config can be entered in a scattergun approach, to some extent at least, as the whole config is picked up at once and not in order. EBNF has obviously been chosen so that debugging a long, unwieldy config file is easier and you might think of the W3 specification for XML being a simple example of EBNF. According to the World Wide Web Consortium (W3C) site (http://w3.org), the formal grammar of XML defines one symbol as so:

```
symbol ::= expression
```

The sudo manual shows some more of these characters and their meanings:

? Means that the preceding symbol (or group of symbols) is optional. That is, it may appear once or not at all.
* Means that the preceding symbol (or group of symbols) may appear zero or more times.
+ Means that the preceding symbol (or group of symbols) may appear one or more times.

You can also see that additions to the config file look as follows:

```
User_Alias      ::= NAME '=' User_List
Runas_Alias  ::= NAME '=' Runas_List
Host_Alias      ::= NAME '=' Host_List
Cmnd_Alias   ::= NAME '=' Cmnd_List
NAME               ::= [A-Z]([A-Z][0-9]_)*
```

And, perfectly sensibly, you can negate a selection with a simple exclamation mark. The manual also informs you that each alias definition is of this form:

```
Alias_Type NAME = item1, item2, …
```

Hopefully, you now have a reference point for the slightly unexpected format of sudo's config. It's actually very clever; for more information on EBNF, refer to the following Wikipedia page: http://en.wikipedia.org/wiki/Extended_Backus%E2%80%93Naur_Form.

Taking Total Control

For unimpeded control of the system, the line that you can see under the privilege specification section means that the "root" user needs this entry to be present.

```
root ALL = (ALL) ALL
```

Loosely translated, this means that the "root" user can execute anything from any terminal and as any user. The actual order is ALL terminals, as ALL users (in parentheses), and the trailing ALL applies to the fact that all commands can be run.

You can also create a Runas_Alias. This is where you are really just create something along the lines of a list of users that you can run commands as. It's important to note that apparently if a Runas_Alias is not specified, then the superuser "root" is assumed. You can declare a UID like this:

```
Runas_Alias OPERATOR = #239005
```

Here, the hash (or pound sign) isn't a comment, but is in fact a UID and acts as identifying a number. This is useful for locking things tightly so there's no ambiguity about the user(s) in question.

Remember that you defined the host CRIX in an early example that "DEVs" were allowed to test stuff on? You declared that as a CIDR-friendly IP address:

```
Host_Alias CRIX    = 10.10.10.10/24
```

You can embellish that entry in order to create an INBOUNDMAIL group of servers, like this:

```
Host_Alias INBOUNDMAIL = courier, dovecot, crix, 10.10.3.4, *.mail.chrisbinnie.tld
```

What about extending the Cmnd_Alias example, too? As you can see, this is powerful too:

```
Cmnd_Alias MAILCMDS = vi /var/qmail/alias/*, nano /etc/postfix/main.cf
```

Aliases Within Aliases

You can also reference your aliases within other aliases to keep the potentially messy config looking cleaner. In fact, you can give lots of varying levels of access to bolster your user access controls.

As the "root" user, you can of course test your configs relatively easily by becoming the user you have offered access to. You can become user "operator" from "root" with something like this command (there are alternatives):

```
# sudo su - operator
```

If you run into any issues, expect to have errors such as this one:

```
Sorry, user operator is not allowed to execute '/bin/bash' as qmail on chrismailserver
```

Finally, in this example, the exclamation mark acts, as you would expect, as a negative:

```
Cmnd_Alias PASSWDS = vi /etc/shadow
chrisbinnie ALL = ALL,!PASSWDS
```

The user chrisbinnie is omnipotent in this case apart from having the ability to edit /etc/shadow.

Troubleshooting

If you get caught out, you can check (logged in as the user in question as just mentioned) which permissions have been assigned to you with the following command:

```
# sudo -l
```

As shown in Listing 13-4, even a low-level user has many settings associated with his environment.

Listing 13-4. An Abbreviated Output of the sudo -l Command

```
Matching Defaults entries for operator on this host:
    requiretty, !visiblepw, always_set_home, env_reset, env_keep="COLORS DISPLAY HOSTNAME
    HISTSIZE INPUTRC KDEDIR LS_COLORS", env_keep+="MAIL PS1 PS2 QTDIR USERNAME
    LANG LC_ADDRESS LC_CTYPE", env_keep+="LC_COLLATE LC_IDENTIFICATION LC_MEASUREMENT
    LC_MESSAGES", env_keep+="LC_MONETARY LC_NAME LC_NUMERIC LC_PAPER LC_TELEPHONE",
    env_keep+="LC_TIME LC_ALL LANGUAGE LINGUAS _XKB_CHARSET XAUTHORITY",
    secure_path=/sbin\:/bin\:/usr/sbin\:/usr/bin
```

If you're interested, the setting !visiblepw apparently relates to sudo refusing to work if passwords are made visible on the terminal on which they're being entered.

133

Summary

This chapter barely scratched the surface of sudo's intricacies. It covered the basics and applied some of them, but mostly explored theory and concepts. There's still a lot of learning required to use sudo as it was intended.

The choice of whether to use sudo is of course yours. Never forget, however, that the "root" account is there for a very good reason. And, don't forget that sudo has its bugs. For some further bedtime reading on sudo, refer to http://www.enterprisenetworkingplanet.com/netsecur/article.php/3641911/Using-sudo-to-Keep-Admins-Honest--sudont.htm.

## CHAPTER 14

Loop Disks and Wubi

Wubi lets you install a few types of Ubuntu Linux (such as Kubuntu or Lubuntu) noninvasively inside a "flat file" that resides in your Windows installation. This chapter discusses Wubi and examines how it works under the hood.

Why Use Wubi in the Enterprise?

Using Wubi in an enterprise environment is not a likely scenario I realize but here is an example where it helped me. Large organizations often insist on providing you with a Windows machine of one type or another—and for good reason. Long ago corporations embraced the plethora of enterprise software available on Windows and have come to rely heavily on it as a result. These businesses also don't want the headaches of having to worry about custom machines for each user. Within large corporations, those that I have worked for at least, if your laptop suffers from some kind of data corruption, rather than attempting to fix it, the pertinent support staff will simply wipe the laptop of all data and then re-image it with a stock-build.

It's not the way I was introduced to computing, but I can see the method behind the madness when two members of staff are responsible for supporting hundreds of laptops; there simply isn't the resource available to spend an hour figuring out a solution to the latest software anomaly unless it affects a large proportion of your user base. You simply revert to your last-known working build and be done with it.

A past employer and I had a brief argument because I insisted that I needed a Linux desktop to work on effectively. Having persisted with my argument for a few days I was eventually given the green light to install one package on my stock Windows 7 desktop with a member of the support team looking over my shoulder. Finally, I had admin access, albeit briefly. The natty little package that I was allowed to install was called "Wubi" (https://wiki.ubuntu.com/WubiGuide).

The premise behind Wubi is super simple. You can install Linux without making any *significant* changes to your Windows operating system. You achieve this by using a *loop* device (also known as a *loop disk*), which is essentially a "flat file" on the Windows filesystem. Yes, the loop disk is just a normal NTFS file. Inside this loop disk, you can make lots of changes without breaking anything on Windows. In essence, you are installing an entire Linux operating system inside a single file. That file includes all the partitions, requisite config and home directories. The only other change (barring a sprinkling of Wubi's tiny associated config files that live alongside the loop disk in a Windows folder) is the addition of another option for you to consider at the bootloader stage. Your choices are therefore whether to boot into Windows as normal or into Linux.

Windows 8 and Wubi

With the introduction of Windows 8, a number of things have changed with the way that Windows sits alongside other operating systems. In a nutshell, Windows simply doesn't play very nicely with other children any more. Apparently the makers of the most popular GUI-based operating system, along with around 140 other tech companies, reached an agreement about how, in the future, our machines should boot up. And as a result, "BIOS" (basic input/output system), which has been used forever to boot up personal computers, has been replaced with "UEFI" (Unified Extensible Firmware Interface). Among a number of improvements, the motivation was to increase boot performance, include options for bigger disks (larger than 2.2 TB), and allow an eye-watering 17.2 billion gigabytes of memory (http://windows.microsoft.com/en-GB/windows-8/what-uefi).

The new-fangled UEFI component which affects Wubi almost certainly relates to the so-called security improvements (which I suspect are actually quite valid). In an attempt to help mitigate "bootkit" attacks at pre-boot time, there are checks and measures now being thrown into the fray. This "Secure Boot" functionality looks like the cause of my fun being spoiled. When using it, only the installed operating system can be booted from correctly.

There's a fair amount of discussion about getting Windows 8 to work with Wubi (http://askubuntu.com/questions/221835/installing-ubuntu-on-a-pre-installed-windows-8-64-bit-system-uefi-supported); for now at least, you should just use older versions of Windows to save your sanity. At some point in the future, I'm (optimistically) sure that there will be a foolproof fix or agreed understanding to allow the operating systems to play nicely together again.

The fact that all dual-boot operating system functionality is affected (and not just Wubi) causes me all sorts of consternation. It means that I need a separate Windows 8 machine (or probably Windows 10—there's more food for thought here http://ubuntuforums.org/showthread.php?t=2255536) to work on in the meantime.

Windows 7 and Wubi

The installation in Windows 7 is so straightforward that I can happily skip through the process of using the stock examples from the official Wubi site. That way you can spend some more time focusing on the good stuff later on, such as troubleshooting and performance tips.

Installing Wubi

To get started, download the Wubi executable from this page: http://releases.ubuntu.com/12.04/. I've picked Ubuntu version "14.04.3" as you can see (codenamed "Precise Pangolin"). This is the latest Long Term Support (LTS) release visible on this page at the time of writing. This is the main landing page for reference: http://releases.ubuntu.com/. The timestamp for that executable file reads "07-Aug-2014 16:04," so check for a newer LTS version if you can.

To install Wubi, double-click the Wubi executable; you'll see a a dialog box similar to the one shown in Figure 14-1. Next, pick a username and password, specify the installation size, desktop environment flavor, and language, and click Install.

■ **Note**   The Wubi web site has a comprehensive Troubleshooting section, which you might want to skim over before committing to an installation, at https://wiki.ubuntu.com/WubiGuide#Troubleshooting.

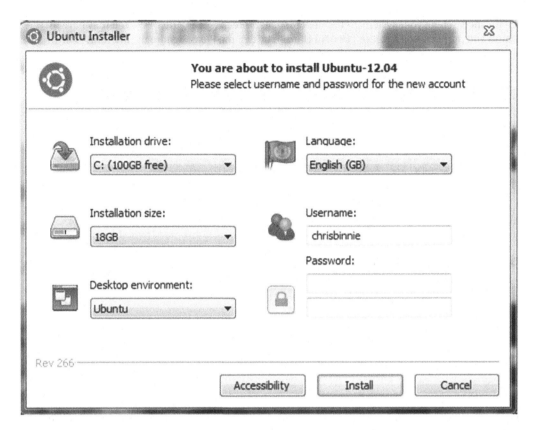

Figure 14-1. The installation graphic found at `https://wiki.ubuntu.com/WubiGuide` *created by contributors to the Ubuntu documentation wiki*

■ **Note**   If you're using your desktop with lots of packages, 8GB of space might not suffice (a *very* loosely defined yardstick is that with loads of packages installed, you might need up to 3.5GB of space plus working space). In the tests on my desktop, I specified my Wubi installation at 12GB; but just as with any Linux build, you can mount other external drives too if need be. Don't go too large as your backups and restore will become too unwieldy to manage.

At this point, you have to wait—about five to ten minutes, depending on your broadband connection and system speed—for an Ubuntu image to be downloaded and installed onto the flat file or loop disk where your operating system will reside.

137

When finished, reboot your system. At the Boot Manager screen (see Figure 14-2), you may have to select Ubuntu and press Enter if it doesn't boot in Ubuntu by default. Please ignore the mention of my favourite Windows version in Figure 14-2, it's only there for added gravitas.

Figure 14-2. *The bootloader graphic found at* `https://wiki.ubuntu.com/WubiGuide` *created by contributors to the Ubuntu documentation wiki*

Should you ever want to remove Wubi from Windows, simply go to Control Panel ➤ Uninstall A Program as you would normally with any other installed program. You can also navigate to the massive file you've created, which can be found in a subdirectory within the C:\Wubi directory (by default) as the file root.disk.

Backing Up Wubi

A Wubi installation only uses flat files. I have a simple script that accesses my 500GB external hard drive and dumps a compressed, timestamp-named backup of the whole Wubi/ directory onto that drive in its various incarnations.

To recover from a crash, I simply boot into Windows and drag the backup folder over to my install directory to restore my entire build. You can easily version, back up, and restore a full operating system. It only takes about 8-10 minutes to restore my test machine to its former glory.

■ **Note**   You might think of these loop disks as a virtualized "containers"—easy to install on Windows 7 (sadly not as easy to install on Windows 8). For more information on containers, refer to https://en.wikipedia.org/wiki/Operating-system-level_virtualization.

Loop Devices

Loop devices are "pseudo-devices". On Unix-like systems especially, it isn't always necessary that software interacts with a physical device, but alternatively they can also access a "pretend" one. You're certain to have heard of other common pseudo-devices such as /dev/null and /dev/urandom, for example.

In the context of Wubi, the software allocates a limited amount of disk space to the application, formats that space with a filesystem, and then installs files into that pseudo-device. This is how many ISO images on compact discs work. When it comes to loop disks the same goes for live CDs, where a whole filesystem can be dropped into a flat file and used as if it was a hard drive or some other physical device with total impunity.

Before you can make use of such a pseudo-device, in the same way that you need to mount a physical device, you also need to run something along the lines of this command:

```
# mount -o loop root.disk /mnt/loopy-loo
```

Here the -o specifies the type of mount as being of the "loop" variety. The loop disk (the massive single file used by Wubi) is called root.disk and is pointed at first. Then the mount point is declared as being inside the /mnt directory. Just like with other drives you would ultimately expose another partition by running the df command; in this case the loop disk being mounted on /mnt/loopy-loo.

In the same vein, when disconnecting from loop disks, use umount:

```
# umount /mnt/loopy-loo
```

You can also employ a useful command to find out which /dev/loopX device has been mounted, where X is a number. The handy command in question is named losetup and it offers the ability to set up and then control loop disks. As well as selecting encryption options or making a loop disk read-only, for example, you can also perform a very useful task, namely resizing a loop disk. However, the Wubi documentation suggests other ways to achieve this, which we'll look at in a second.

The losetup manual offers a concise example of creating a loop disk, encrypting it using the "DES" (Data Encryption Standard) cipher, and then mounting it, having formatted it (see Listing 14-1). Note, however, that using DES is "painfully slow," whereas an alternative, XOR, is sadly very weak. Stick with DES in this instance.

Listing 14-1. Manually Creating a Loop Disk, Encrypting It, and Mounting It

```
# dd if=/dev/zero of=/file bs=1k count=100
# losetup -e des /dev/loop0 /file
<now enter your password>

# mkfs -t ext2 /dev/loop0 100
# mount -t ext2 /dev/loop0 /mnt
```

In Listing 14-1, I use the dd command to create a loop disk, losetup to set it up, mkfs to format it (using the ext2 filesystem), and then finally mount it as ext2.

Once you have finished using your loop disk, you can then unmount it using "delete" with -d (also known as "detaching") with these simple commands:

```
# umount /dev/loop0
# losetup -d /dev/loop0
```

I will leave you to experiment with the other available creation and deletion options. In Figure 14-3, you can see the switches that can be used with the excellent `losetup` command.

```
Usage:
 losetup loop_device                              give info
 losetup -a | --all                               list all used
 losetup -d | --detach <loopdev> [<loopdev> ...] delete
 losetup -f | --find                              find unused
 losetup -c | --set-capacity <loopdev>            resize
 losetup -j | --associated <file> [-o <num>]      list all associated with <file>
 losetup [ options ] {-f|--find|loopdev} <file>  setup

Options:
 -e | --encryption <type> enable data encryption with specified <name/num>
 -h | --help              this help
 -o | --offset <num>      start at offset <num> into file
      --sizelimit <num>   loop limited to only <num> bytes of the file
 -p | --pass-fd <num>     read passphrase from file descriptor <num>
 -r | --read-only         setup read-only loop device
      --show              print device name (with -f <file>)
 -v | --verbose           verbose mode
```

Figure 14-3. *How the losetup command uses its available options*

With your new loop disk, you could mount it and then treat it as a new drive for testing (which can be readily broken) or copy the contents of an existing image such as a DVD to it.

Wubi Tips

Now that you have successfully installed Wubi and understand a little more about how it works, there are a few things that you need to consider.

After your installation has completed, you should first boot into Windows and run `defrag.exe` in order to encourage your disk to function as speedily as possible. If you want an alternative to the built-in version of defragmentation software found in Windows, then you might want to try this: `http://www.kessels.com/JkDefrag/`.

If you're not constantly changing your Ubuntu settings, backing up your initial entire Wubi installation, even just once after you're happy with it, will suffice. And, if your work habits are similar to mine, then you probably won't even be booting into Windows much and therefore have an opportunity to break it. If all else fails, run through the usual `chkdsk` command prompts and let Windows recover so that you can boot into Ubuntu again. This is at least one thing that modern Windows builds achieve relatively reliably.

The other gotcha is also in relation to Wubi being sensitive to power outages. This is because, whether you're using Wubi or not, Windows is not great at recovering from just switching the power off at the wall or a power cut. This doesn't just apply to Windows of course—try to avoid such scenarios altogether if you can. At home I use a tiny UPS, which protects against power surges too, and as a result these types of power issues tends to only happen if I kick the power cable by accident.

You can choose to copy your existing disk into another newly created one (that is larger than your current one) or you can opt to boot off of a live CD and resize your loop disk in the true sense of the description. Both methods are explained here: `https://help.ubuntu.com/community/ResizeandDuplicateWubiDisk`. I found the first method perfectly adequate; just take your time so you don't break anything and be sure to back up your entire `root.disk` beforehand.

Another approach is to separate a partition, such as the /home partition, away from your main loop disk in order to free up some well-needed space. The Wubi web site provides for more information on this approach; in a nutshell, you want to download the wubi-add-virtual-disk tool (https://wiki.ubuntu. com/WubiGuide?action=AttachFile&do=view&target=wubi-add-virtual-disk) and then run the following command to achieve the required results:

```
# sh wubi-add-virtual-disk /home 25000
```

In this example, 25000 is the size of the loop disk in MB that your /home directory will reside in. If I chose this method, then I would be tempted to make this loop disk relatively large and back up the new /home loop disk less often. I would use some other tool to back up your important /home files more frequently.

In addition to resizing your Wubi loop disk, you also have the option to convert your not-so-pseudo Ubuntu build into a fully fledged installation. It's not the easiest thing to do in the world but if you're feeling brave and don't have any more spoken-languages left to learn, you can attempt it using the instructions found here: https://help.ubuntu.com/community/MigrateWubi.

You can of course (carefully, so that you don't delete the Windows installation directory or break it in some unrecoverable way) also access your Windows files via Wubi's installation, which I find very useful.

If you're using the Nautilus File Manager, finding your Windows NTFS files is as simple as navigating to the /host directory via the "Computer/File System" section.

■ **Tip** For other useful Wubi tips refer to the "Misc." section on the official Wubi site at https://wiki.ubuntu.com/WubiGuide#Misc.

Summary

If you weren't aware of Wubi already then hopefully this brief insight will generate enough enthusiasm for you to give it a try. On Windows 7 and older versions, its installation is quick and innocuous. It is also very easy to uninstall and the software is unquestionably mature, so there's really very little risk to your Windows build. I encourage all levels of users to familiarize themselves with it. As you've seen, it installs without any invasive issues and disabling it is simply a case of removing the bootloader entry.

If you decide to write a simple script in order to provide a quick desktop-backup solution, you're almost certainly also going to want to try using containers (did I mention that you really should try out OpenVZ (https://openvz.org)?!). The whole premise of having portable machine images is the direction that computing has been moving in for some time. And, combined with cloud technologies, it's unquestionably a skill worth getting your head around.

APPENDIX A

■ ■ ■

Hack, Break, Fix

While the security industry is constantly evolving its countering techniques, the categories of attacks suffered since the inception of the Internet have rarely changed. Both White Hats and Black Hats, whether testing with good intentions or nefariously attacking networks and systems respectively, generally only learn about a handful of different categories of attacks.

Understanding the many attack vectors that an attacker will target is of paramount importance for any White Hat. This appendix explores putting an older tool to good use on today's Internet. The fact that you can safely attempt exploits yourself and understand how to guard against them means that this invaluable tool rates very well in comparison to other security tools.

Step forward "Damn Vulnerable Linux" (known as DVL). If you want to learn about hacking, plugging security holes, and fixing broken systems, then to my mind the excellent DVL is still definitely worth looking at.

Exploring DVL

The DVL web site was taken offline around 2011 allegedly because it threatened to breach German security laws. Despite that, DVL was one of the most useful security technologies anyone interested in Linux could explore over the past few years.

You are actively discouraged from installing DVL onto a hard drive, so I will presume that you can configure your own VirtualBox (https://www.virtualbox.org), Virtual Machine (VM), or some other type of container. Alternatively, you can use DVL on its own live CD (without any permanent installation at all) or at a push you might have a suitably old machine whose drive can be happily wiped.

If you visit the SourceForge download URL mentioned there and then look at the list of ISO files, you can see a list of a few different DVL versions.

The link at the top saying "Looking for the latest version?" might suffice. There was a mention of the developer(s) working on version two of DVL and that link mentions bt2final.iso. If that's not working for you, you should have some success with downloading "DVL_1.5_Infectious_Disease.iso".

Once DVL is installed, you will see a screen mentioning the venerable BackTrack Linux (which is sadly now obsolete and its site now effectively points at Kali Linux; see https://www.kali.org), depending on your version. Following the onscreen instructions, you should then be able to log in using credentials such as these:

```
Login: root
Password: toor
```

Figure A-1 shows the basic GUI desktop manager of DVL version 1.5, despite a massive part of the work you will do on DVL being command-line based (in a shell).

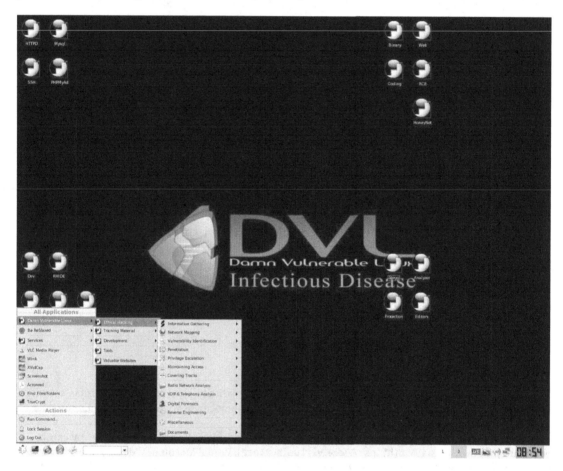

Figure A-1. *An image showing the DVL desktop manager as found on the DistroWatch site; see*
`http://distrowatch.com/images/cgfjoewdlbc/dvl.png`

By using older, more vulnerable, kernel versions, DVL can increase the attack surface of your VM considerably. You can definitely have a field day with some of the puzzles and exploitable software. Among the mountain of goodies, for example, are some nasty SQL (Structured Query Language) injections you can explore.

Lots of the system functions are purposely broken in varying degrees, such as the networking config. In terms of the packages, however, you can experiment with older versions of a web server (Apache), PHP, Database Server (MySQL) and an FTP server. You can also play with GCC (GNU Compiler Collection) and `strace`, among many other compiler packages, to your heart's content.

The former DVL web site made a big deal about not being able to cheat because there were no solutions provided. It's a nice claim and improves your bragging rights when you've achieved a hard-won level of success. Let's have a look at some of the applications bundled with DVL (without giving much away at all to avoid spoiling your fun).

Figure A-2 shows a sample of the bundled software that's designed to keep you on your toes.

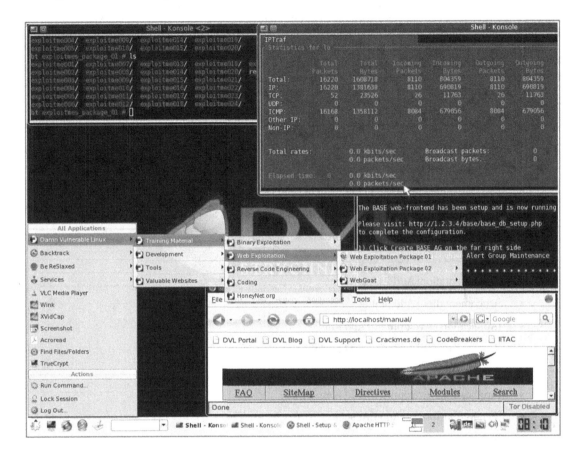

Figure A-2. *A snapshot from the DVL's Wikipedia page*

Depending on the version of DVL you are using, you should be confronted with a couple of web browsers (Firefox and Konqueror), some useful documentation (follow Damn Vulnerable Linux from the Start button), and a quick and easy access to a shell.

With a little digging, you can also look through a veritable treasure trove of utilities such as disassemblers and debuggers. If you've ever come across something called "breakpoint testing" or used watchpoints, these are exactly the tools that will assist you.

What's in the Box

As I've alluded to, the excellent testbed that is Damn Vulnerable Linux offers a number of different facets for you to hack, break, and fix. A number of very useful tutorials are also included. Previously, there were a number of videos on the DVL web site to complement these docs, but you might struggle find them online now.

Apparently around 65% of us are "visual learners," which means that we will respond best to learning from graphics and charts. There are a few users showing off their DVL skills and the odd sample can be found on YouTube it seems, but at a glance the original videos aren't available. The Wayback Machine can only offer so much after all (`https://archive.org/web`).

An excellent site called VulnHub (see `https://www.vulnhub.com/series/damn-vulnerable-linux,1/`) has a comprehensive list of that and is included in the DVL releases. For example, according to VulnHub in DVL version 1.4 (codenamed "Strychnine"), you can expect to find the following contents:

- [Application Development] Add Motor IDE

- [Application Development] Update HLA to 1.98 and StdLib to 2.3

- [Application Development] Add LogWatch

- [DVL Core] Add XEN

- [Reverse Code Engineering] Add Insight GDB Debugger

- [Tutorials] Add CPU Sim - An Interactive Java-based CPU Simulator

- [Reverse Code Engineering] Add JAD Java Decompiler

- [Tools] Add VLC Media Player

- [Documentation] Add TeTex

- [Documentation] Add JabRef

- [Application Development] Add Kile

- [Documentation] Add kDissert Mindmapper

- [Peneration Testing] Add JBroFuzz

- [Application Development] Add WebScarab

- [Peneration Testing] Add CAL9000

- [Reverse Code Engineering] Add KDBG

- [Application Development] Add xchm

- [DVL Core] Add gtk libs

- [Tools] Add xvidcap

- [Tools] Add AcroRead

- [Tools] Add Scite

For a teaser (I promised not to discuss details for good reason), the following list shows what was included with DVL v1. This release was apparently only a collection of tools from which the VM could be further developed on as opposed to hacking, breaking, and fixing VM.

- HT 0.5

- libreadline4_4.2a-5_i386

- gdb_5.2.cvs20020401-6_i386

- binutils_2.12.90.0.1-4_i386 (including objdumps,gas,strings ...)

- nasm-0.98-1.i386

- HLA v1.86
- libelfsh0-dev_0.65rc1-1_i386
- elfsh_0.65rc1-1_i386
- Apache 2.0.5.4
- Php 4.4.0
- ethereal-common_0.9.4-1woody12_i386
- ethereal_0.9.4-1woody12_i386
- libpcap0_0.6.2-2_i386
- tcpdump_3.6.2-2.8_i386
- lsof_4.57-1_i386
- ltrace_0.3.26_i386
- nmap_2.54.31.BETA-1_i386
- strace_4.4-1.2_i386
- ELFkickers-2.0a (including sstrip, rebind, elfls, ebfc, elftoc)
- GCC/G++ 3.3.4
- GNU Make 3.80
- bastard_bin- 0.17.tgz
- Mysql-server 4.4.1
- Ruby 1.8
- Python 2.3
- lida-03.00.00
- DDD 3.3.1

Vulnerable

It is difficult to ignore the VulnHub site. If you're ever lost for a hobby, you could do worse than lose a weekend or two using some of the VM images on VulnHub. It's a collection of pre-built images, among other things, that you are encouraged to exploit. Here's an example of a stated goal as found on the "Acid: Reloaded" VM: "Escalate the privileges to root user and capture the flag".

You might also want a look at this demo if SQL exploits interest you. It's called "codebashing" (http://www.codebashing.com/sql_demo) and the site talks about learning about securing your applications. There are paid-for options and the site promises that programmers will teach you all about the ever-important application security.

A community project that aims to allow users to upload sandbox applications for others to hack is aptly named https://hack.me. What I like about this site is the diverse variety of what it calls "hackmes". If you visit https://hack.me/explore then there's web forms, PHP bugs, and other varieties available. There's a "hackme" called "Delete All The Things," which kindly requests that you use SQL injections to delete the entire users table in the database. The nicely built site is certainly worth a look and adding a contribution to if you're feeling inclined.

It seems that Java is all the rage at the moment. There's a purposely-insecure J2EE (Java 2 Platform Enterprise Edition) application that aims to help teach security concepts called WebGoat (https://www.owasp.org/index.php/WebGoat_User_Guide_Table_of_Contents). Once you have Tomcat up and running, you are asked to do the following with each security assessment:

- Examine client side content, such as the HTML and scripts.

- Analyze communications between the client and server.

- Review any cookies and other local data.

You simply point your local browser at http://127.0.0.1/WebGoat/attack to get started. You can use these credentials to gain access:

```
Login: guest
Password: guest
```

Along the same vein, you could probably get lost in WebGoat for a number of days.

Finally, here's a piece from back in the day (written in 1999), which looks at a Buffer Overflow that exploits a program with SUID permissions. It's well written and provides insight into what goes on behind the scenes during an attack (or at least what used to go on back in the year 1999); see http://www.linuxjournal.com/article/2902.

Summary

You could probably soak up a number of days attempting to exploit, harden and repair some of the code and VMs that we've looked at. There are literally thousands of security tools available to both attackers and those who want to protect their systems.

If you haven't seen the likes of these tools before, it's improbable that you will be immediately able to step into a career in penetration testing or become a security professional. You should, however, be armed with a number of very useful tools that help to get you part of the way there. If you are interested in this area, you could do much worse than have a look at the excellent, comprehensive package called Metasploit (http://www.metasploit.com). It provides a framework that helps inject exploits into remote machines in order to essentially monitoring how they react. You work with payloads and choose which bug to take advantage of, among other aspects. There's also an eye-opener of how to encode your attack traffic so that firewalling (intrusion detection systems) ignore the payload as it is presented to their filtering rules. All in, it's potentially a very complex tool but a fantastic learning experience that will take you one step further than many other available tools.

Hopefully, your arsenal now includes enough extra security weaponry to help you do more than the bare minimum to keep your services running.

Index

Get the eBook for only $5!

Why limit yourself?

Now you can take the weightless companion with you wherever you go and access your content on your PC, phone, tablet, or reader.

Since you've purchased this print book, we're happy to offer you the eBook in all 3 formats for just $5.

Convenient and fully searchable, the PDF version enables you to easily find and copy code—or perform examples by quickly toggling between instructions and applications. The MOBI format is ideal for your Kindle, while the ePUB can be utilized on a variety of mobile devices.

To learn more, go to www.apress.com/companion or contact support@apress.com.

Apress®
THE EXPERT'S VOICE™

All Apress eBooks are subject to copyright. All rights are reserved by the Publisher, whether the whole or part of the material is concerned, specifically the rights of translation, reprinting, reuse of illustrations, recitation, broadcasting, reproduction on microfilms or in any other physical way, and transmission or information storage and retrieval, electronic adaptation, computer software, or by similar or dissimilar methodology now known or hereafter developed. Exempted from this legal reservation are brief excerpts in connection with reviews or scholarly analysis or material supplied specifically for the purpose of being entered and executed on a computer system, for exclusive use by the purchaser of the work. Duplication of this publication or parts thereof is permitted only under the provisions of the Copyright Law of the Publisher's location, in its current version, and permission for use must always be obtained from Springer. Permissions for use may be obtained through RightsLink at the Copyright Clearance Center. Violations are liable to prosecution under the respective Copyright Law.

Printed in the United States
By Bookmasters